Praise for *Andy Pruitt's Complete Medical Guide for Cyclists*

"If a cyclist can do only one thing to improve his or her riding experience, it should be adjusting the bike, shoes, and saddle to fit better. The absolute authority on this topic is Dr. Andy Pruitt. Andy combines leading scientific research, more than three decades of experience, and an unbridled passion for cycling into an unparalleled ability to improve any rider's experience on the bike.

"Throughout most of my life, I experienced recurring knee pain; Andy assessed my problem, and in a matter of minutes, he corrected the misalignment that was causing the issue. My knee is now pain-free, even after back-to-back six- or seven-hour rides.

"Whether it's eliminating pain, increasing power output, or boosting efficiency on the bike, every cyclist can benefit from Andy's knowledge and expertise."

—MIKE SINYARD, founder & president of Specialized Bicycles

"For almost 30 years now, Andy Pruitt has been 'The Man' for myself and many, many other cyclists of all ability levels, especially when it comes to the myriad issues involved in defining optimal bike fit or making the correct diagnosis to either prevent or treat injuries. For me, Andy's engaging and easily understood book stands alone."

—DAVIS PHINNEY, former U.S. Pro national champion
& 7-Eleven team member

"Having worked with elite-level cyclists for nearly 20 years, Andy Pruitt is a medical expert cyclists can rely on. He has helped me recover from many injuries over the span of my career. His wealth of experience with elite-level cyclists has made him one of the foremost medical experts in cycling."

—DEDE DEMET BARRY, world & national champion road cyclist

D1044399

ANDY PRUITT'S
Complete Medical Guide
for Cyclists

ANDY PRUITT'S
Complete Medical Guide for Cyclists

ANDREW L. PRUITT Ed.D.

with **FRED MATHENY**

VELO.
press

BOULDER, COLORADO

The information in this book is intended for educational and instructional purposes. It is not intended to replace medical care, rather to be adjunct to it.

VeloPress®, a division of Inside Communications, Inc.
1830 North 55th Street
Boulder, Colorado 80301–2700 USA
303/440-0601; Fax: 303/444-6788; E-mail: velopress@insideinc.com

To purchase additional copies of this book or other VeloPress books, call 800/234-8356 or visit us at velopress.com.

Distributed in the United States and Canada by Publishers Group West.

Cover and interior photos by Don Karle; cover design by Elizabeth Watson
Interior design by Trish Wilkinson; interior illustrations by Ed Jenne
Models: Scott Tietzel, Kristin Hilger, and Neal Henderson

Library of Congress Cataloging-in-Publication Data

Pruitt, Andrew L.
    Andy Pruitt's complete medical guide for cyclists / Andrew L. Pruitt with Fred Matheny.
        p. cm.
    Includes index.
    ISBN-13: 978-1-931382-80-9 (pbk. : alk. paper)
    ISBN-10: 1-931382-80-8 (pbk. : alk. paper)
    1. Cycling—Health aspects. 2. Cycling—Physiological aspects. 3. Cycling accidents. I. Matheny, Fred. II. Title.
RC1220.C8P78 2004
617.1'0270247966—dc22

                                                                2005031464

Printed in the United States of America
10 9 8 7 6 5 4 3

CONTENTS

PART II
REMEDIES FOR CYCLING INJURIES

PART III
GETTING THE MOST OUT OF CYCLING

FOREWORD

I FIRST MET ANDY PRUITT IN 1981 WHEN I WAS A YOUNG RACER suffering from a stabbing pain along the side of my knee. Andy was the head athletic trainer at the University of Colorado, and for Boulder's expanding population of elite athletes, he was rapidly gaining a reputation as the medical professional to see if you had overuse injuries that no one else could fix.

Andy told me I had iliotibial band friction syndrome. It was the first time I'd ever heard this term. With his treatment, the symptoms vanished quickly. But unlike other medical pros I had seen, Andy was more interested in what was *causing* my symptoms. He carefully checked my position on the bike and modified it. I never had that injury again.

All through his career, Andy's focus has been on finding and preventing the causes of injury.

When I started coaching, I sent my U.S. National Cycling Team athletes to Andy. Over the years, he worked with Lance Armstrong, Bobby Julich, Marty Nathstein, Tyler Hamilton, Chann McRae, Fred Rodriguez—all the riders who are at the top of the sport today.

His medical expertise is now legendary. He pioneered video analysis to determine bike fit. He has worked with Lance to increase his flexibility so he can achieve a more aerodynamic time trial position. The 1994 world's were in Sicily, where it was extremely hot. Karen Kurreck was suffering from dehydration, but Andy solved the problem and Karen won the World Time Trial Championships.

Andy was never too busy to help. He never turned away an athlete because his appointment roster was full or failed to return my phone calls because he was too involved with his own practice.

Andy can take his own advice, too. When we went to Colombia for the world championships, he set up a detailed program so the riders wouldn't get sick. It worked. The cyclists stayed healthy. Andy didn't get sick, either—but he spent most of his time treating the staff. We had been so busy telling riders not to drink the water that we had forgotten to take care of ourselves!

Above all, Andy always puts the athlete first.

He was the Chief Medical Officer for U.S. Cycling when we were preparing for the 1996 Olympics. We wanted to use narrow bottom brackets on our time trial bikes for better aerodynamics, so Andy devised force-measuring pedals to see if riders could produce as much power with their feet closer together than in their normal stance.

But Andy wasn't just interested in power production. He also wanted to see if a narrow stance would cause injuries that might lead to long-term problems. He was looking beyond the riders' performances in Atlanta and focusing on their health for the rest of their lives. That approach is the measure of the man.

I'm happy that Andy has finally compiled his knowledge about cycling injuries in a book. He is unique among the world's cycling medicine experts because he can diagnose and treat cycling problems for everyone—recreational as well as elite cyclists.

If you love to ride and want to continue for your whole life, the information in this book is priceless.

Chris Carmichael
President of Carmichael Training Systems

PREFACE

by Andrew L. Pruitt, Ed.D.

As I write this preface, I am on Lufthansa Flight 447 bound for Florence, Italy, to meet up with Damiano Cunego, the winner of the 2004 Giro d'Italia, and his Lampre team. Yes, this is the ultimate house call. I certainly do not do this for just anybody, and Lord knows, I cannot see every achy knee in my clinic at the Boulder Center for Sports Medicine, which is the exact reason I wrote this book. With the help of my longtime friend and teammate, Fred Matheny, I tried to compile my three decades of experiences with cyclists of all ages and levels into a complete medical advice guide. The purpose of the guide is to help all of you train injury free, ride in comfortable and powerful positions, and heal from the inevitable injury faster. Without underestimating the complexities of the human body and the bicycle, I have tried to keep the information easy to understand but medically accurate.

The concept of scientific bike fitting has grown in popularity over the life of my career. It makes me smile when I see and hear things concerning bike fit that I originally said, but was not smart enough to claim with copyrights, trademarks, or patents. I have always offered my experiences, both scientific and anecdotal, openly in lectures, magazine articles, and text. I too have borrowed from other notables within the cycling industry. In this text I have added the advice of some of my close colleagues, as well as cutting-edge, if not controversial, information on the aging process from a "world's leading authority."

It is my sincere hope that you find this book informative and maybe even entertaining.

PLEASE READ THIS!

BICYCLING IS A POTENTIALLY DANGEROUS ACTIVITY. CRASHES AND accidents with motor vehicles are possible. Death can result. Bikes can exceed fifty miles per hour on descents. But even slow-speed crashes can lead to serious injury.

Some of you may decide to race or ride in large groups on tours or charity rides. Riding in a pack presents additional dangers. Because some riders aren't as skilled or as careful as others, they can involve you in a crash.

Please be careful while riding. Always wear a helmet, gloves, and eye protection. Obey traffic laws. Don't get caught up in the excitement of the moment and ride dangerously, whether in a race, event, or training ride. The information in this book will help you avoid overuse injuries, but it can't protect you from crashes caused by inattention, equipment failure, or other dangers you will meet on bike paths, streets, and highways.

We hope you want to enjoy the
wonderful sport of cycling for many years.
Do it safely with a full understanding
and acceptance of its dangers.

INTRODUCTION

by Fred Matheny

As Chris Carmichael noted in his foreword, the advice and wisdom in this book comes from Andy Pruitt's medical training and years of experience working with elite and recreational cyclists.

Andy Pruitt's Medical Guide for Cyclists was so popular that, as time passed and Andy's medical advice evolved, it became time for a revision. Just one measure of the book's popularity are cycling physicians who come to see Andy about their medical problems or for a bike fit often carry a well-worn personal copy, passages illuminated with highlighters and pages dog-eared for ready reference. They use Andy's book for their own cycling ailments as well as those of their patients.

Andy and I worked together to add material to the book that was originally left out due to space limitations. We also included the latest findings from many of Andy's colleagues at the Boulder Center for Sports Medicine and experts he has met in the course of his practice.

In addition to these revisions, we have added six completely new chapters to give you a more complete medical guide to cycling. The new material covers crucial issues such as biomechanics, designing your own training program, and how to find the Holy Grail of comfort combined with performance. There's also a chapter on stretching and rehabilitation for cyclists, so if you get injured, you can work to get well.

To convert Andy's knowledge into book form, I spent hours interviewing him (on and off the bike) over the course of several years. Working with him also gave me the opportunity to attend numerous medical conferences on subjects like orthopedics and cardiology, thus giving this English major a substantial medical education.

Andy Pruitt is simply the most experienced and most expert bike fit authority in the United States, if not the world. For twenty-five years, he has studied how the human body should sit on a bicycle for maximum comfort as well as to produce the most power.

In addition, he has ministered to thousands of cyclists—from riders like us to elite performers, including Lance Armstrong. There's no quirk of anatomy affecting bike fit that Andy hasn't seen. No fit-related cycling injury has passed by him unnoticed.

If you come to the Boulder Center for Sports Medicine for a bike fit, Andy and his colleagues will take as much time as needed to fit you properly. They won't rush. But it's fascinating to watch Andy do a bike fit at cycling camps where he has to fit many people in a limited time. He puts a rider on the trainer, watches them pedal for a minute or two, and inevitably nails the problem. "I bet your right hip hurts," he'll say, and a look of wonder crosses the cyclist's face. "How did you know that?" Andy knows, and can spot problems quickly, because he's worked with so many cyclists and because he has thought deeply about how the human body interacts with a bicycle.

Cycling is not an injury-prone sport. Unlike running, it's nonimpact. Many riders go through whole careers with only minor aches and pains. Although cycling is generally easy on the body, things sometimes go wrong. Overuse, poor bike fit, badly designed training programs, crashes, aging—all can lead to injury.

Because of this, there's a saying in Boulder, Colorado: "You'll eventually have to see Andy." You can go early in the course of an injury and get it fixed quickly, or you can wait until it becomes chronic. But one way or the other, many riders end up at the clinic Andy directs. They sit in a waiting room with walls festooned with bikes hanging on hooks and autographed jerseys of great riders, including Lance Armstrong, Christian Vande Velde, Julie Furtado, Andrea Peron, Connie Carpenter, and Dede Demet Barry.

Andy helps everyday cyclists, too. I credit him for my own continued ability to ride. In late 1994, I injured my knee skiing powder on a tree-covered slope. It didn't seem too bad and I skied the rest of the day. After all, lift tickets are expensive. But over the next month, the pain worsened and became more debilitating. That's when I went to Andy. He and his orthopedic associate at the time, James Holmes, M.D., performed an arthroscope. They found damage to the articular cartilage on the end of my femur, the sort of injury that could eventually lead to a knee replacement, especially on a knee that had been previously injured in college football.

Here's where Andy and Jim's extensive experience with athletes saved the day. Formerly there had been no good treatment options. But they knew about a relatively new procedure (from 1995) called micro-fracture. It worked, and I've been riding and hiking ever since.

It was only several years later, after Andy was sure the procedure had been a success, that he told me the prognosis for this injury for people over 40 is quite poor. His skill helped me beat the odds.

What if you don't live near Colorado? Simply read this book and follow Andy's advice. It just may save you a trip to Boulder.

ANDY PRUITT'S
Complete Medical Guide
for Cyclists

PART I

BIKE FIT

CHAPTER 1

BIKE FIT RULES

Cyclists are often obsessed with bike fit. The more experienced they become, the more they worry about the subtle differences that a couple of millimeters can make. And for good reason.

Eddy Merckx, considered by many to be the greatest cyclist who ever lived, carried a 5 mm Allen key in his jersey pocket. He is famous for making slight adjustments in saddle height, often several times a day. Sometimes he even raised or lowered his saddle while riding the bike during races. It's often said that Merckx was persnickety about bike fit because he suffered nagging pain resulting from injuries in a crash. But he also had an undetected physical abnormality that gave him problems throughout his entire cycling career.

Awhile back, Eddy brought his son Axel to my office. (Axel now rides for the Phonak team and is an excellent pro in his own right.) I examined the young rider and found a significant inequality in leg length primarily in his femur, or thighbone. Incredibly, Eddy has the same problem.

When I diagnosed this, Eddy realized why he had been so uncomfortable on the bike despite his great success. At the thought of all the pain he had suffered—pain that could have been alleviated with a properly shimmed and adjusted cleat—he remarked, with his characteristic rueful grin, "Where were you when I was riding?"

Merckx's constant fiddling with bike fit points to what all cyclists know. If you're uncomfortable, riding is no fun. Additionally, bike fit is closely connected to power production, and no one wants to squander even one watt of hard-earned power due to a poor position on the bike.

Bike fit is a hot topic right now. As riders age, getting comfortable on the bike is a much higher priority than it was when they were 25, limber, and so eager to ride that pain didn't matter. But just because the average age of cyclists is increasing doesn't mean they aren't interested in going fast. So along with comfort, cyclists are seeking a position that allows them to get the most power possible. (For more information, see Chapter 17.)

The importance of having good bike fit is now recognized among cyclists. These days you can find fit systems and fit experts everywhere—on the Web, on your local club ride, or at your bike shop. Some of these systems and experts are well qualified and will do a great job of setting you up on your bike properly. Unfortunately, not all are as qualified. Recommendations from these so-called experts can be just plain incorrect, and

FIGURE 1.1 Andy fitting a rider at the Boulder Center for Sports Medicine.

following their guidelines can lead to loss of power, discomfort, and injury. You may see a "medical bike fit" offered, but this is intended for riders with preexisting medical conditions and is not what most riders need.

Finding an expert (see Figure 1.1) to help you get a good bike fit is definitely a case of "buyer beware." Fortunately, it isn't hard to find your ideal riding position. There are a few simple rules to remember about finding the bike fit that is right for you.

RULE 1: BIKE FIT IS A MARRIAGE BETWEEN BIKE AND RIDER

When I give talks about bike fit to physicians or cyclists, I often describe a cyclist dressed in wedding garb with his bike on the steps of a church. It's a visual way of reminding people of the importance of compatibility between bike and rider. Marriage is a strong metaphor for the partnership of human and machine, but it's an apt one. In fact, serious riders may spend more time with their bikes than with their spouses!

If you and your bike are incompatible, the marriage will fail. Just as married couples must adjust to each other, so must a bike and rider. However, a bike can be adjusted in multiple ways; the saddle can be moved up or down or the stem can be changed to suit the anatomy of the rider as needed. But the body can be adjusted only in minor ways—with a carefully designed stretching program and by adapting to progressively longer rides. This leads us to the second rule.

RULE 2: MAKE THE BIKE FIT YOUR BODY, DON'T MAKE YOUR BODY FIT THE BIKE

It's easy to adjust a bike but difficult to stretch or contort your body into some preconceived "ideal" position. Therefore, it's important to focus on making the bike fit you, rather than your trying to match the way another cyclist rides. For example, if you have long legs coupled with a short torso and arms, your bike should have a relatively short top tube and stem combination (often called "reach"). But if you have stubby legs and most of your height is in your torso, you need a long top tube and stem.

Many riders get their idea of perfect fit from watching pro riders in person, in videos of races, or in magazine pictures. Then they try to emulate riders they admire. This is a bad idea for many reasons. Pro riders are usually lean and lightly built. If you're not quite as svelte, it's hard to get as low and aerodynamic as a pro who isn't bending over a middle-aged paunch. Even a fit and lean 50-year-old is probably not as flexible as a 130-pound, 22-year-old professional rider.

The pros are also generally quite flexible because they've been riding competitively since they were young. Their bodies have had time to adapt to extreme positions that result from the handlebars being much lower than the saddle.

Finally, pros compete in as many as 100 races a season. Much of their riding from February to October is spent at the intense levels required by racing. It's easier to maintain a low and aero position when going hard; it's much more difficult when cruising at a recreational pace. When you cycle hard, pedaling levitates your body slightly off the saddle and you lean over into the effort. But when you're cycling at a moderate pace, you tend to sit up, which puts pressure on your hands and your seat. As a result, you'll feel poor fit faster than the hardworking pro.

So forget what your favorite pro rider's bike looks like unless your body and your riding style are carbon copies of his. Make your bike look like you, not like your hero.

RULE 3: DYNAMIC BIKE FIT IS
BETTER THAN STATIC BIKE FIT

Most bike fit systems are static; that is, adjustments are made with a rider sitting motionless on a trainer or from a set of formulas using body part measurements. An example is the LeMond Method (see Chapter 2), which establishes saddle height and frame size from a measurement of the distance from the pubic bone to the floor.

There's nothing wrong with these static methods of bike fit. Static and numerical formulas are an important starting point from which we can move to dynamic fit. But any static formula is only a starting point.

When you are pedaling, you are constantly moving on the bike. As you pedal, you actually rise or levitate slightly from the saddle. Therefore, the adjustments made when you're sitting motionless will result in a different saddle height than if measurements are taken while you are pedaling. Reach to the handlebars can change, too. When you're cruising, it's easier to reach brake lever hoods that are a bit too far away from the saddle. But when you're riding hard, the hamstrings and muscles in the lower back tighten with the effort, making the bars seem farther away. Every rider has experienced this phenomenon of the bike "growing" as the ride gets longer. It's one reason that while climbing, we tend to sit up and grab the tops of the bars next to the stem.

At the Boulder Center for Sports Medicine, we use a dynamic system to determine bike fit variables such as saddle height. First, we attach reflective markers to specific anatomical landmarks on the rider's knee, ankle, and hip (see Figure 1.2). Then we put him on the trainer and have him pedal.

We use movement-capture hardware and software to take pictures of the pedaling rider. The camera emits infrared light to pick up light from the reflective markers, which are sensitive to infrared. A computer converts the rider into a 3-D stick figure. From that data we can determine exact and functional fit for saddle height, saddle fore/aft, and reach to the bar.

When we first developed this system, all the computerized information had to be entered by hand. Additionally, the bike frame got in the way of the leg farthest from the camera, so its position had to be inferred. It often took hours to get the data. But now the technology is much more sophisticated. Results are essentially instantaneous. We can have a rider converted to a pedaling stick figure almost as soon as she is off the bike. Finding the ideal bike fit now is just a matter of minutes, rather than hours.

Again, there's nothing wrong with static bike fit and mathematical formulas as a starting place. In fact, in this book I'll suggest a number of ways to find ballpark figures for these important measurements. For 95 percent of riders, the information in this book will enable powerful and pain-free cycling. But if you're constantly uncomfortable on the bike or beset with nagging injuries, there's no substitute for an anatomical dynamic bike fit done while you're actually pedaling.

RULE 4: CYCLING IS A
SPORT OF REPETITION

A basketball player probably won't get an overuse injury from shooting. Even if he hogs the ball and puts it up every time he touches it, that probably results in only about thirty repetitions of the shooting motion in a game. And once his teammates are onto him, he probably won't get the ball as much!

But cycling, by its nature as an endurance sport, demands continual repetition of the same pedaling motion for the duration of the ride. At a cadence of 90 revolutions per minute, a 6-hour century ride requires 32,400 iterations of the pedal stroke for each leg. That's a lot of repetition!

Worse, each pedal stroke is almost identical. Your knee tracks in the same plane when observed from the front, and it bends the same amount at the top of each stroke. As a result, a minor misfit (for instance, having the saddle too low by several millimeters or having one leg longer than the other by just 5 mm) can lead to major problems over time. That's why fit is so important.

Cycling's repetitive nature manifests itself in the areas of hydration and nutrition too. Training requires about 600 calories per hour, and racing may burn upwards of 1,000 calories per hour. The best conditioned rider can store glycogen for only two hours of hard effort. This means that only halfway through a century ride, you're dehydrated and malnourished! It's not just your connective tissue that suffers on long rides.

RULE 5: REMEMBER THE FIT WINDOW

There is a window of good fit on a bike for each rider. I don't want to make bike fit sound like a matter of millimeters. Everyone is different, and even with all my experience I can't tell you exactly how high your saddle should be or nail precisely your best reach to the handlebars without much study of your particular situation.

FIGURE 1.2 The rider is prepared to do a 3-dimensional bike fit with infrared markers on the knee, ankle, and hip.

Most standardized bike fit systems will get you within 2 cm of this fictional "perfect" fit. At the Boulder Center, we can get a little bit closer. But over time your body will lead you to make adjustments that bring you within this "fit window" of a centimeter on either side of your virtual "perfect" measurement. If you are presently comfortable on your bike, that's great. If not, keep working at finding a better position.

RULE 6: MOUNTAIN BIKES
ARE AN EXCEPTION

These rules apply to road bike riders as well as people who ride a mountain or hybrid bike on the road. When riding on a road, your position stays relatively the same, and you spend a low percentage of the time out of the saddle. Therefore, repetitive forces are high when riding on the road.

However, riding a mountain bike on technical terrain like rough singletrack or rocky four-wheel drive roads lessens the repetition somewhat. Instead of pedaling with the same motion for hours, you're bouncing all over the saddle, standing to get over obstacles, and descending with the pedals horizontal while using your arms and legs as shock absorbers.

Because of this, fit on a mountain bike is a bit different from fit on a bike ridden predominantly on the road. For instance, many off-road riders like their mountain bike saddles about 1 cm lower than they set seat height on their road bikes. The lower saddle provides a bit more power for high-torque climbing and makes quick dismounts easier.

But remember the "fit window" of 2 cm. Even if you ride off-road exclusively, getting a good road fit helps. A good road fit can serve as a baseline reference. Then you can make modifications for riding off-road from a solid starting point.

CHAPTER 2

SADDLE POSITION

SADDLE POSITION IS THE KEY FIT VARIABLE AND THE MOST important measurement to get right. Both saddle height and saddle set-back are important.

If the saddle is too low, the knee is bent excessively at the top of the pedal stroke where power production begins. As a result, there's too much shearing force on the back of the patella (kneecap) where it tracks in a groove in the femur (thighbone). A low saddle also produces compressive forces behind the knee. Because the knee joint never gets to "unfold," the pressure on the back of the patella is constant. Problems can develop in the kneecap that can be quite painful.

Conversely, a saddle set too high can cause pain to develop behind the knee. In this case, the rider has to reach too far at the bottom of the pedal stroke, excessively stretching the hamstrings. A high saddle also compromises power production. A cyclist's leg is like a lever, and the patella is the fulcrum. The more the leg straightens, the less effective the power output becomes. When your knee bend is about 15 degrees, the patella loses contact with the femur entirely. (At 0 degrees, the leg is straight.) When the saddle is too high, the patella is no longer an effective fulcrum, and power output suffers.

Another problem that can result from excessive saddle height is an increased risk of saddle sores and crotch irritation. When the saddle is too high, you have to reach farther to keep your foot on the pedal. With

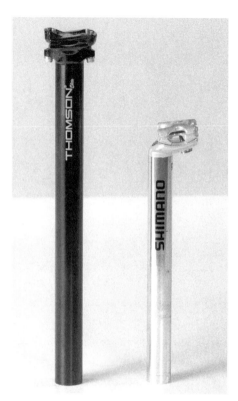

FIGURE 2.1 The Thomson seatpost (left) has no setback; the Shimano post (right) has this feature.

modern clipless pedals, your foot does not rise off the pedal at the bottom of the stroke—it's fixed. If the stretch is too far, your body compensates by rocking the pelvis across the saddle on each pedal stroke. The soft tissue of your crotch gets strummed across the nose of the saddle eighty or ninety times per minute. It is easy to see how this can cause painful irritation.

Some cyclists have made the height adjustment but have not considered setback. This important variable controls where you sit in relation to the bike's bottom bracket (the center of crank rotation). To make the adjustment, slide the saddle forward or backward along its rails on the seatpost. A rider with long legs will need to position the saddle farther back; a rider with short legs will need to slide it forward. Riders with very long or short legs may have a hard time getting a good fit. The saddle rails may not be long enough, limiting adjustability. If this is your situation, look for a saddle that has rails with more room for adjustment— that is, rails with longer straight sections. Also, on some seatposts the clamp is situated farther back, behind the middle of the seatpost, allowing the saddle to be moved farther to the rear (see Figure 2.1).

The last adjustment to saddles that you should consider is the tilt. Saddles can be tilted up or down or be completely level. As you'll learn later in this chapter, in most cases, your saddle should be level, and riding with it tilted can be an indication that something else on the bike is not properly fit and should be adjusted.

SADDLE HEIGHT FOR ROAD BIKES

To find the correct saddle position for a road bike, the first thing you should adjust is the saddle height. There is a simple way to find the ideal saddle height for you. Place the bike on a trainer, and pedal for five minutes in a medium gear. This loosens up your muscles and allows your body to get positioned on the saddle where you normally sit. Then unclip your shoes and place both heels on the pedals. Pedal slowly. Pay attention to your knee bend at the bottom of each stroke: If your saddle is at the correct height, your knees should be fully extended at the bottom of each stroke as you pedal with your heels. Your heels should almost, but not quite, lose contact with the pedals as they go around the bottom. Your pelvis should remain level with no hip rocking. If your knees are not fully extended at the bottom of the pedal stroke, or if your heels lose contact with the pedal entirely, adjust the height of the saddle up or down as necessary, and repeat this test to check your adjustment.

When you clip into the pedals after the height is properly adjusted, the balls of your feet are located over the pedal axles. This extra length results in the appropriate amount of knee bend as you pedal at the bottom of the stroke.

Some cycling shoes have raised heels to make walking easier. Pedaling on these raised heels will alter this measurement method. If your shoes have visible heels, try pedaling with your instep (where the sole of the shoe is thinner) on the pedal to determine the right saddle height.

The LeMond Method
Another method you can use to find the right saddle height was popularized by three-time Tour de France winner Greg LeMond. It's an approach that Greg learned from his French coach, Cyrille Guimard. This method was in wide use ten or fifteen years ago, but it has slowly been supplanted by newer techniques. However, it's referred to often among cyclists and cycling experts, so it's worth knowing.

For this method, you'll need a carpenter's square, record album, or large, thin book; a measuring tape; and a friend to help you. First, in bare feet and wearing cycling shorts, stand with your back against a wall.

Place your feet about six inches apart. Put the carpenter's square (or record album or book) between your legs with one side flush against the wall and the other side sticking out in front of you. The top edge should be parallel to the floor. Raise the carpenter's square until the pressure you feel against your crotch is equal to the pressure you feel from a saddle when you're pedaling easily. Hold it there and have a friend use a measuring tape to measure from the top of the horizontal edge of the carpenter's square to the floor. Record this crotch-to-floor distance precisely in centimeters. Multiply this number by 0.883.

The result is the proper height, in centimeters, for your saddle, measured from the center of the bottom bracket axle to the top of the saddle along the seat tube. For instance, if your crotch-to-floor measurement is 87 cm, your saddle height should be 0.883×87, or 76.8 cm.

There are a few drawbacks to this formula that riders must take into consideration. It was developed in the early 1980s when equipment was different. Cycling shoes had thicker soles, and pedals with toe clips positioned the foot higher above the axle than modern clipless pedals do. Because of this difference, if you're using modern equipment, the 0.883 multiplier may be too high. However, you can still use it as a good starting point for establishing a ballpark saddle height, and then fine-tune the adjustments using the method described earlier.

Riders with long feet in proportion to their height may find that this formula results in a saddle that's too low. Long feet have the effect of lengthening legs beyond standard proportions. This formula may also result in a saddle too low for cyclists with excessive soft tissue over their sit bones. Sitting on the saddle for a while causes that soft tissue to compress, which must be taken into account. Getting the correct saddle height for these riders requires a more practiced eye on the part of the fit technician.

Additionally, some choices that cyclists make about their clothing can effect the correct saddle height. Wearing shoes with added thickness, such as thicker insoles or cycling-specific orthotics that extend under the ball of the foot, effectively lengthens your legs. This requires a higher saddle. In contrast, adding thickness between your crotch and the saddle, for example, wearing thick winter cycling tights, effectively shortens your legs and requires the saddle to be slightly lower.

Using a Goniometer

Another way to measure saddle height is to use a goniometer, a device that is similar to a protractor, to measure the angle of the knee when the pedal is at the bottom of the stroke. Most riders produce optimum power, with the least chance of injury, when the knee angle is between 25 and 35 degrees.

The fit technician aligns the goniometer on three specific anatomical landmarks: the bony bumps at the hip (greater trochanter), the knee (approximate center of rotation of the knee), and the ankle (lateral malleolus) (see Figure 2.2). You can get a goniometer to check your own saddle height online at www.lemondfitness.com.

FIGURE 2.2 Andy uses a goniometer to measure knee flexion at bottom dead center.

SADDLE HEIGHT FOR MOUNTAIN BIKES

If you frequently ride your mountain bike on pavement or smooth dirt roads for long periods of time, use the guidelines given above for road bikes to determine the saddle height for your mountain bike.

There are two exceptions. Measure the crank arms—the arms that connect the pedal to the bottom bracket axle. If the crank arms on your mountain bike are longer than the crank arms on your road bike, lower the saddle an amount equal to the difference in crank arm length. This is necessary to give you the correct amount of bend in your knee at the bottom of the stroke. For example, if you run 170 mm crank arms on your road bike but 175 mm on your mountain bike, lower your mountain bike's saddle 5 mm.

If you normally ride on technical terrain, saddle height isn't as important, because you aren't locked in one position pedaling many repetitions like you would be on the road. On technical terrain you move around on the saddle and get out of the saddle frequently, making precise measurements of saddle height useless. Because of this you may want to lower the saddle as much as 1 cm from the height recommended for a road bike.

FRAME SIZE

Getting the right frame size is important too. Frames that are too large may not have enough standover height (the distance from the ground to the top of the tube) for sudden dismounts. Because frames are designed with proportional top and seat tubes, a frame that is too high may be too long as well.

The crotch-to-floor measurement you got using the LeMond method to find the correct saddle height will help you find your frame size, too. Follow the directions on pages 15–16 to find your crotch-to-floor measurement in centimeters. Then multiply this measurement by 0.65. For example, if your crotch-to-floor distance is 87 cm, then multiply 87 by 0.65 to get 56.5 cm. This means you should ride a frame that measures between 56 and 57 cm.

Frames are measured along the seat tube from the center of the bottom bracket to the top of the top tube. However, many modern-day frames don't have the traditional diamond shape with a top tube parallel to the ground, and it can be hard to find the center-to-top measurement on newer frames. Most manufacturers give a "virtual seat tube height" measurement for bikes that are designed with angled top tubes. This makes it easy to choose the correct frame size without awkward measuring.

In the past, frames were designed to allow a large gap—as much as three inches or more—between the handlebars and the top of the saddle. Now we've come to realize that bars set higher, sometimes almost even with the saddle, can improve comfort and power production without compromising aerodynamics. So frame builders have designed bikes with a higher front end or extended head tubes to make it easier to move the bars higher. However, if you need your handlebar fairly high compared to the saddle for comfort, you probably need a larger frame than the above method would suggest. In that case, use 0.7 as a multiplier to find the right frame size. Use this higher multiplier also if you have a relatively long torso or arms and need a frame with a longer top tube. Frames with longer top tubes also have longer seat tubes.

SADDLE SETBACK

The saddle setback refers to the forward or backward location of the saddle on the seatpost. The most important factor in determining the correct setback is the length of the cyclist's femur (thighbone). The saddle setback should put your knee's center of rotation directly over the pedal axle of the forward crank arm when it's horizontal. When everything is adjusted properly, the wide part of the saddle will be directly under the sit bones (ischial tuberosities) to give you maximum support.

Correct setback is important for two reasons. First, it positions your knees so that you can drive power directly into the pedal at the point in the crank circle where it does the most good. To get maximum power from the pedals, the center of the knee's rotation must be directly over the ball of the foot (and therefore the center of the pedal axle). (Some riders may not have their cleats directly under the balls of their feet, because of problems like hot foot or because they prefer the greater leverage that a rearward cleat provides.) And second, correct setback positions your hips so they are neither too far forward nor too far behind the bottom bracket. Either of these extremes can cause injury or chronic pain as you pedal.

Before you check saddle setback, set the correct seat height. Then follow the guidelines here to adjust the setback. Adjusting the setback may change saddle height slightly, so you'll need to recheck it afterward.

To determine correct saddle setback, make a plumb line by tying a heavy washer or nut to one end of a piece of string. You will need a friend to help take this measurement.

1. Put your bike on a trainer. If the surface isn't level, shim the legs of the trainer until it is. Pedal for five minutes to warm up and find the place on the saddle where you normally ride.

2. Stop pedaling, leaving the crank arms horizontal (parallel to the floor) and your right foot forward. Take care not to raise or lower your heel when you stop pedaling. Have your friend watch to be sure it's in the same position as when you were turning the crank.

3. Your friend should drop the plumb line from the front of the kneecap on your right leg (see Figure 2.3). The line should touch the end of the crank arm. If the line falls in front of or behind the end of the crank, loosen the seatpost bolts and slide the saddle forward or backward on the rails as necessary.

FIGURE 2.3 Dropping the plumb line in front of the kneecap to the end of the crank arm.

4. Pedal for a minute to reestablish your normal position on the saddle, then recheck with the plumb line and readjust the setback, if necessary. Keep at it until you get it right. Be patient—this is an important measurement.

5. Once the plumb line touches the crank arm when hanging along the front of the kneecap, switch feet so your left leg is forward. Have your friend drop the plumb line from the front of the left kneecap. If the line doesn't touch the end of the crank arm like it does on the right side, you might have an inequality in femur length. In this case, adjust the saddle setback to split the difference.

Some authorities say that the plumb line should be dropped from the bony bump *below* your kneecap (called the tibial tuberosity). The line should then bisect the pedal axle when setback is right. I prefer to use the front of the kneecap because it's an easier anatomical landmark to find. Also, the bony bump varies in thickness and location among individuals, making this a less precise way to measure. Finally, it's easier to see if the plumb line touches the end of the crank arm than it is to judge its relationship to the pedal axle. The end results are very similar.

Changing the saddle's position forward or backward can change its height. If you had to slide the saddle a considerable distance to achieve proper setback, recheck the saddle height. If it needs to be changed, adjust it and then check setback again. You may have to adjust both setback and seat height alternately until both are correct.

Remember that on some seatposts the clamp is located farther back, behind the middle of the seatpost, so you can slide your saddle farther back. If you have longer legs, be sure to shop for a seatpost with the setback you need.

CAUTION! *It's a fashion statement in some cycling circles to have the saddle jammed as far back on the seatpost as possible so the rider can sport what he considers a "pro" position. But this setback is right only for riders with long femurs and flexible lower backs and hamstrings.*

EXAMPLE: *Greg LeMond has extremely long femurs. His kneecaps seem to be only slightly above his ankles! For him, a bike with a slack seat tube angle, a long top tube, and the saddle jammed all the way back is appropriate. Such a position puts his knees over or just slightly behind the pedal axle.*

But most people aren't built like Greg. Former pro Ron Kiefel, a seven-time Tour de France competitor, once moved his saddle back when a famous rider he admired told him he'd be faster if he did. Ron didn't get faster. Instead, he developed severe back pain and missed several weeks of racing.

The moral of this story: Let your femur length, not your hero, determine your saddle position.

SADDLE TILT

At mass-participation cycling events like centuries or Ride the Rockies, you'll likely see a lot of variations in saddle tilt. Some riders have the nose pointed down at extreme angles—as much as 30 degrees. Other riders tilt the nose so high that their saddle looks like a jumbo jet taking off. It's painful to look at.

Here's the rule: If you're a recreational or touring cyclist and you ride with the nose of your saddle pointing up or down, your bike doesn't fit. The reach to the handlebars is probably incorrect.

In general, your saddle should be positioned level with the ground. It should not be angled up or down. Check it with a carpenter's level or by placing a yardstick lengthwise on the saddle and comparing it to something horizontal, such as a tabletop or windowsill.

Incorrect saddle tilt can often help diagnose other problems with fit. If your saddle is tilted with the nose up, it may mean that your handlebars are too far away and too low. If your saddle were level, you'd tend to slide forward to reach the bars and find yourself always scooting to the rear to compensate. Riders with this problem often tip the nose up to keep them from sliding forward. The tipped-up saddle is a tip-off to the poorly positioned bars. (See Chapter 3 to learn how to adjust the handlebar position and reach.)

There can be other problems with incorrect saddle tilt. If the nose of the saddle is down, you'll place too much weight on your arms and hands as you try to stop your body from sliding forward. The result may be arm fatigue and numbness in your fingers. Downward-sloping saddles also put too much of your weight on the front wheel, which degrades bike handling. Additionally, tilting the saddle down doesn't solve crotch problems like numbness or excessive saddle sores. Instead, it can make them worse. When you're constantly sliding down the saddle and then pushing yourself back, crotch irritation results.

If the nose of the saddle points up, it will push against the soft tissue, blood vessels, and nerves in your crotch. This leads to saddle sores, numbness, and the risk of erectile difficulties (in males). When the nose points up, it also has ramifications for the lower back. The normal curvature is changed, often resulting in pain.

Despite these risks, there are two exceptions to the level-saddle rule. Cyclists with unusual pelvic tilts or lumbar postures (swayback, for instance) sometimes require a slight upward tilt (1 to 3 degrees) so they can get their weight on their sit bones rather than on soft tissue. Posture irregularities don't have to be so pronounced that they're noticeable. A very subtle swayback syndrome that tilts your pelvis forward as you lean over to hold the handlebar could cause pain. But usually a simple adjustment—raising the handlebar slightly—will let you level the saddle and still take the pressure off the pudendal nerves in your crotch.

And in rare instances, the saddle should be tilted down slightly. This is appropriate mainly when you're riding in a low time trial position with aero bars. With aero bars, considerable weight is borne on the forearms, which tends to keep the pelvis centered on the saddle even if it's not completely level.

CHAPTER 3

HANDLEBAR POSITION

ANOTHER IMPORTANT ASPECT OF BIKE FIT IS THE POSITION OF the handlebars, commonly called *reach*. Proper handlebar fit is an important part of preventing arm and wrist pain or numbness.

Reach is a combination of top tube and stem length in relation to how far forward or backward the saddle is located on the bike. The reach to the handlebar determines the angle of your torso in relation to the ground. The shorter the reach, the greater the angle. Touring cyclists sit relatively upright, while time trialists want their backs to be almost parallel to the ground. The torso angle that's best for you will depend on the way you ride, your goals in cycling, your body's limitations, and your comfort.

Other contributors to reach are the type of brake levers you have and the shape of your handlebars. The shape of the bend in the brake levers can affect where you grip the lever hoods, which changes the reach. Some handlebars are longer from front to back, which results in a longer reach. Some have a deeper drop, or downturn, than others. All of these factors must be taken into consideration as you determine the best reach for you.

Reach is the most individual part of bike fit. It depends on a wide range of factors including hamstring and lower-back flexibility, lower-back strength, posture, arm and torso length, and shoulder strength. Each of these factors also plays a role in determining the height of the bar in relation to the saddle. Age is part of the equation, too. As we get older, we often lose flexibility regardless of how much stretching we do. The handlebar has to be raised, and often the reach must be reduced to fit our bodies as they age.

Most bikes built before the early 1990s used conventional quill stems and threaded steerer tubes, and adjusting handlebar height was relatively easy. All you had to do was raise or lower the stem. But with the advent of threadless headsets, which are more common on newer bikes, handlebar height adjustments became more complicated.

> **TIP:** *If you're buying a new or custom bike, don't let the shop cut the steerer tube until you're sure the fit is right.*

REACH TO A DROP HANDLEBAR

For bikes with a drop (or downturned) handlebar, there are a few different methods you can use to approximate correct reach to the handlebar. You can use these to determine what height the handlebar should be compared to your saddle. These simple guidelines are useful starting points.

> **CAUTION!** *Be sure your saddle height and setback are correct before you adjust the handlebar.*

The first method is from an old Italian wives' tale. To determine reach, put your elbow against the tip of the saddle and extend your open hand toward the handlebar. Position the handlebar so it is within an inch or so of the end of your middle finger. Make additional adjustments after a few rides if necessary.

Another method you can use to get a ballpark estimate of the proper relationship of handlebar height to saddle height is to measure your fist across the knuckles from little finger to index finger. Adjust the stem of the handlebar so that the difference between the top of the bar and top of the saddle is equal to your fist measurement. Take several rides, then make adjustments based on feedback from your body.

CAUTION! *These anatomical approximations assume that all of your body parts are in proportion. Is there a relationship between the size of your fist and the length of your upper body? Or the flexibility of your lower back? Sometimes—but not always. Still, these approximations provide a good starting point.*

A third way to determine reach is to measure how your weight is distributed across the bike. Your reach to the handlebar should be such that 40 percent of your weight is on the front wheel and 60 percent is on the rear wheel. However, there's no good way to determine those percentages. One way to estimate this is to use two bathroom scales. Put the bike's rear wheel on one scale and the front wheel on another. Then sit on the bike and check the scales. Is 40 percent of the combined weight registered on the front scale? This is a rough approach at best because it's done while you're stationary rather than pedaling.

REACH TO A FLAT HANDLEBAR

Some road riders prefer a flat handlebar, which positions the rider more upright. This is especially useful if you're using a bike for commuting, since sitting upright gives you better control on busy streets.

It's easy to duplicate your drop-bar reach when you convert to a flat bar. This method also works for determining the correct reach on a mountain bike.

1. Put some blue carpenter's chalk on the web between your thumb and index finger.
2. On a road bike that is properly adjusted, pedal on the trainer for several minutes. Then measure the distance from the tip of the saddle to the blue chalk mark you left on the brake hoods.
3. With the blue chalk still on your hands, ride the bike with the flat handlebar and note where the blue mark appears on the grips. The distance from the tip of the saddle to the chalk marks should be the same on both bikes.

If you want to set the reach on a flat bar bike like a mountain bike and don't have a road bike to use for comparison, simply set the mountain bike bars so the angle of your back to the ground is about 45 degrees or slightly more (see Figure 3.1).

HANDLEBAR HEIGHT

As we've seen, the differential between the height of the saddle and the height of the handlebars can have a pronounced effect on comfort and power production. In general, both bar height and reach should be adjusted so your torso angle fits within the following guidelines:

Racers and competitive recreational riders: torso angle of 30 to
    45 degrees
Fitness riders: torso angle of 40 to 50 degrees
Casual riders: torso angle of 50 to 60 degrees

> **CAUTION!** *Flexibility matters. If you can't stand with locked knees and bend over to touch your toes after only a minimal warm-up, none of the static bike fit formulas will work for you. None of them! You'll need a higher handlebar, set closer to the saddle.*

> **EXAMPLE:** *At the Boulder Center for Sports Medicine, we recently diagnosed a young pro with a congenital back ailment. He has since raised his handlebar almost 3 inches. He went from a 12 cm bar/saddle differential to about 5 cm. He still looks like a pro on the bike, and he's amazed at the increased comfort.*

If you're riding a bike with aero bars (which protrude from the front of the handlebar) and spend most of your time on them riding fast and hard, these formulas don't work. With aero bars, you can ride in a lower position with your back more horizontal without putting undue stress on your hands, arms, and lower back, because by resting your forearms on the aero bar pads, you take the strain off these areas.

FIGURE 3.1 Andy uses a goniometer to measure the torso angle of a competitive rider.

Remember that even if you had your bike fitted by someone with extensive training and experience, that doesn't guarantee the reach will be right the first time. Because of all the variables that go into it, it's beyond even the best bike fitter's skills to get reach right on the first try. This dimension is just too personal because of anatomical variables that are not obvious to the bike shop fitter.

As a result, don't feel shy about returning to the shop if you realize after riding several hundred miles that you need a stem change. Riding for several hours can pinpoint areas of discomfort that weren't obvious in the shop the first time. Finding the right reach is a precarious balance, and a good bike shop will understand this and help you get the fit you need.

HANDLEBAR WIDTH

Handlebars come in several widths. Some manufacturers measure drop bars from the center of the bar ends, while others measure from the outside of these openings.

Generally, the bar on your road bike should equal the width of your shoulders, using the center-to-center handlebar measurement (see Figure 3.2). To determine your shoulder width, have a friend measure from one acromioclavicular (AC) joint to the other. The AC joint is the prominent bump located on top and about two inches from the outside of each shoulder (refer to Figure 8.2 on page 85). The distance between these two (in centimeters) is the same-width handlebar you should use.

Criterium specialists—riders who compete in group races consisting of multiple laps—may prefer a narrower bar so they can more easily squeeze through tiny openings in the pack.

Long-distance riders usually like wider bars for more comfort and steering stability. Wider bars aren't a panacea, however, because they can create their own set of physical problems. Wide bars spread out the hands and put undue stress on the elbows and shoulders. Women usually have narrower shoulders and less upper-body strength to help them cope with ill-fitting bars.

FIGURE 3.2 Correct handlebar width.

BRAKE LEVER PLACEMENT

A traditional drop handlebar—one positioned with the flat lower portion pointing to the bike's rear brake—should be nearly level when viewed from the side. However, styles have changed, and many of the new designs in anatomic handlebars are often positioned so they're rotated up, with the flat lower portions pointing down below the rear brake. This raises the brake levers in relation to the top of the bars and also accommodates the nontraditional bar shape so it's more comfortable.

Once you've set the handlebar height correctly, you're ready to position the brake levers. To do this:

1. Hold a straightedge under the flat part of the drop bar so that it projects forward (see Figure 3.3).
2. Move the lever on the bar until the tip just touches the straightedge.

This is the lowest you should position the brake levers. However, you might find that you prefer them to be higher. Many riders, even pros, find comfort with the levers placed slightly higher on the bar curve.

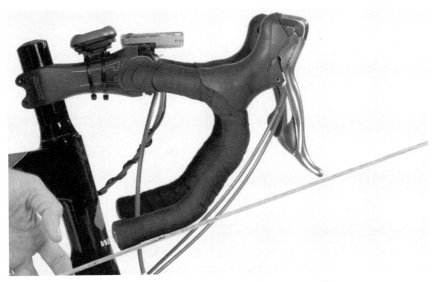

FIGURE 3.3 A straightedge helps position brake levers correctly.

Anatomical handlebars that have flat sections in the bends for hand comfort may vary the fit somewhat. If you have this type of bar, follow this general rule: Position the levers so you can reach them equally well from atop the hoods or in the drops.

Touring or long-distance cyclists may want to rotate the bar in the stem so the drops point at the rear hub rather than the brake. This raises the top of the lever hoods, putting them closer to the saddle to create a more upright position.

Different brands of brake levers have different fits. Shimano models have a more abrupt transition from the lever body to the handlebar compared to Campagnolo brake levers. Some riders find one brand or the other to be more comfortable.

If you're updating from brake-only levers to combination brake/shift levers, remember that brake/shift levers have bodies about 1 cm longer to accommodate all the internal mechanisms. As a result, you need a stem 1 cm shorter.

It's fine to position one brake lever slightly different than the other. Remember, the bike should look like you. Some riders have one arm that's slightly shorter than the other as a result of a broken bone or congenital factors. A broken collarbone can cause the same effect. In these cases, you'll want to position the brake lever higher on the side with your shorter arm.

> **TIP:** One signal that you need an asymmetrical reach is a stabbing pain behind one shoulder blade or on one side of your neck. Check by riding a trainer. Have a friend look from the front and from behind to see if your shoulders are level. Adjust your brake levers until they are.

HAND POSITIONS ON A DROP BAR

The shape of drop handlebars has remained basically the same for a hundred years. There's a good reason for this apparent lack of innovation—the standard downturned shape is best suited for comfort and control. It provides a number of hand positions, too. This is crucial because leaving your hands in one place guarantees numb and tingling fingers.

There are three primary hand positions on a drop bar.

On the lever hoods. Position your hand so that the web between your thumb and index finger is atop the brake lever hood with the thumb to the inside and the four fingers to the outside (see Figure 3.4). Curl your index finger across the top of the lever. Keep your wrist straight. From this position, it's easy to brake with one or two fingers and shift if you have combined brake/shift levers. This is also the standard position for out-of-saddle climbing.

If you have levers with concealed cables, one useful variation on this position is to put the middle of your palm on the tip of the hood as if you were resting your hand on the end of a cane.

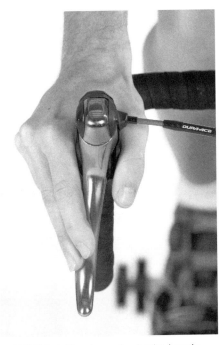

FIGURE 3.4 Hands on the brake hoods illustrating a neutral "handshake" position.

This stretches you out slightly and aids aerodynamics. When the reach is correct, your forearms will touch the top of the handlebar, providing support, comfort, and aerodynamics.

FIGURE 3.5 Holding the bars on the tops near the stem.

On the tops near the stem. Place both hands, palms down, on the handlebar beside the stem (see Figure 3.5). Some riders prefer to move their hands farther out, near where the bar begins to curve forward, for additional stability. This is the standard climbing position. It allows you to sit more upright to get more power and make breathing easier. Many riders also use it for easy cruising because of the upright position.

If you need to ride one-handed (while drinking from your water bottle, for instance), use your one hand to hold the bar near the stem. If you hit a bump or are jostled from the side, you're less likely to swerve. This works because the closer to the bar you put your hand, the less leverage you have for steering. A bump isn't likely to make you jerk the bar.

> **CAUTION!** *You'll sometimes see a racer reach back to grab a teammate's hand and sling him forward on a climb or into a better position for a sprint. The racers hold their bars near the stem for better stability. But don't try this move unless you know exactly*

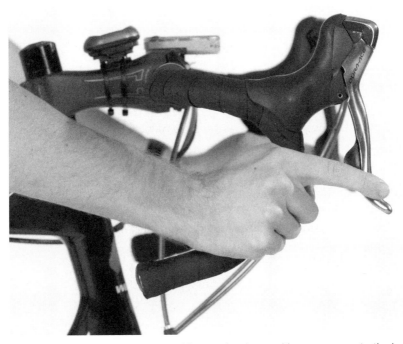

FIGURE 3.6 Comfortable hand position on the drops with easy access to the brakes.

what you're doing. It's an easy way to tangle the bikes and take your friend down with you.

On the drops. Grip the low section of the bar near the curves ("hooks") for descending or fast, flat riding (see Figure 3.6). This is the most aerodynamic position on a drop handlebar. This grip also produces the most powerful braking because you can pull on the levers with several fingers while opposing the force with your thumb wrapped around the bar.

Some riders defy conventional wisdom and grip the drops during out-of-saddle climbing. They argue that this provides more leverage for them to get their upper body into the pedal stroke. Climbing in the drops used to be discouraged on the grounds that the bent-over posture makes breathing difficult and aerodynamics don't matter going uphill. But top climbers like the late Marco Pantani were often seen on the drops in the 1990s, so more riders are trying it. And they do seem to be going faster.

TIP: *No matter which grip you use, remember to change it frequently. If your bike fits properly, holding the bar tops will be as comfortable as riding in the drops. If you are comfortable with your hands in only one location, it's a sign that your reach to the handlebar is incorrect.*

CAUTION! *Some riders install a long stem with the bar much lower than the saddle, thinking that this makes them look like a pro. But the reach is often so excessive that they have to ride most of the time on the tops with their hands next to the stem. Then they have to move their hands each time they want to brake or shift.*

Modern brake/shift levers are designed to reward riding with the hands on the lever hoods, where both shifting and braking are readily accessible. This is, to use a computer term, the default position. Still, it's best to change your grip every few minutes to avoid hand numbness.

AERO BAR POSITION

Aero bars can be attached to most drop handlebars (see Figure 3.7). They aid comfort and improve aerodynamic efficiency. But they also can be quite dangerous if you use them in a group or paceline: Your control of the bike isn't as sharp, and your hands are a long way from the brake levers.

There are only two situations in which you should install aero bars on your road bike. First, they're useful for long-distance cycling when you're riding many miles solo or with just a couple of other riders. Install the aero bars so when you're on

FIGURE 3.7 Aero bars produce a narrow position to slice through the wind.

them, a plumb line dropped from the front of your shoulder exits at the back of your elbow. In other words, your upper arm should be nearly vertical, with the elbow slightly ahead of the shoulder.

Second, aero bars are useful for riding time trials, when getting low is less important than getting narrow to improve aerodynamics. Adjust the armrests so your arms are within the width of your hips when viewed from the front. Use a mirror or have a friend check. Also, slide the saddle forward 1 to 2 cm depending on what's comfortable and how much power you can produce (see Figure 3.8).

For a pure time trialing position, first adjust the saddle's height and setback, then position the aero bars so that when you drop a plumb line from the front of the forward knee, it falls 2 cm in front of the end of the crank arm when it's horizontal.

FIGURE 3.8 Time trial bikes optimize the rider's aerodynamics.

CHAPTER 4

PEDALS AND CLEATS

THE LAST ASPECT OF BIKE FIT TO CONSIDER IS THE PEDAL SYSTEM. Having the proper pedal fit can help eliminate foot and knee pain, as well as help you increase the amount of power you're able to get out of the bike.

Modern clipless pedals are a significant innovation compared to the clips, straps, and slotted cleats of just a few years ago. With clipless pedals, there's no pressure across the instep caused by toe straps; there are no toe clips digging into the end of your toes. Clipless pedals are easy to enter and exit. In a crash, your feet automatically disengage so you aren't attached to the bike as you fall.

Clipless pedal systems have, however, made bike fit more important. With slotted cleats, if one leg was slightly longer than the other, the cleat on the short leg could rise a bit off the pedal rail at the bottom of the stroke to compensate for the inequality. The small amount of play in toe straps, even when pulled fairly tight, also helped.

But with clipless pedals, your foot is locked into the pedal by the cleats, and no compensation is possible. Over many repetitions of the pedal stroke, a poor fit can lead to problems such as lower-back pain.

Adjusting pedals and cleats is supremely important. Here's how.

FORE/AFT FOOT POSITION

The first thing to consider is how far forward or back your foot is positioned on the pedal. In general, the ball of your foot should be directly

FIGURE 4.1 Correct cleat placement under the ball of the foot.

over the centerline of the pedal axle. This is considered a neutral position (see Figure 4.1). The ball of the foot is the first metatarsal phalange joint—located directly behind the big toe. While wearing your shoes, feel for the ball with your finger, then mark the side of your shoe where it's located. Align the mark with the center of the pedal axle. Adjust the cleats by sliding them forward or back on the shoe until you get it right.

This placement works best for men's size 9 feet (European sizes 41–42). Riders with longer feet will need more stability and should move the cleats farther back on the shoe to put more of the foot in front of the pedal axle. In contrast, riders with shorter feet may need more lever length and thus should move their cleats more toward the front of the shoe so they are pedaling more "on their toes."

The options you have for placement of the cleats will vary by shoe model. Each shoe manufacturer drills the same hole pattern for several shoe sizes. If you're at the extremes for the hole pattern (because you have long or short feet), it may limit your ability to put the cleats in the optimum position.

You may find that there are certain instances in which you need to change the position of the cleats. Long-distance riders often find that they can avoid painful numbness and hot foot—a burning pain in the ball of the foot—by sliding their cleats all the way back on the shoe. This puts the balls of their feet as far ahead of the pedal as possible, thus avoiding direct pressure on the ball of the foot. In fact, some ultramarathon riders go so far as to drill more holes in the shoe soles so they can move their cleats even farther to the rear. (For another solution to the hot foot problem, see Chapter 7.)

EXAMPLE: *Race Across America legend Lon Haldeman's business is taking riders across the United States on his PAC Tours— transcontinental rides that average well over 100 miles a day. (Go to www.pactour.com for more information.)*

Sometimes a rider will develop such extreme foot discomfort that it's hard to continue. When this happens, Haldeman drills their shoes and moves their cleats as much as 2 cm farther back. This usually provides an instant cure, with pain-free pedaling the rest of the tour.

Many ultramarathon riders claim that this modification doesn't diminish the power or suppleness of their pedal stroke, so they ride with their cleats to the rear all the time. However, this contention has yet to be tested in the lab.

CAUTION! *Drilling shoe soles is a last resort. Don't try it until you've exhausted the other remedies for hot foot in this book. Drilling can ruin expensive shoes if you don't know exactly what you're doing. In some soles, drilling additional holes can weaken them. Also, moving cleats far to the rear may reduce hot foot symptoms but create other physical problems as the body copes with the extreme change in position.*

ROTATIONAL CLEAT POSITION

Some riders' feet point in or out from the centerline of the bike. In addition to the fore/aft setting, cleats can be rotated to accommodate these foot postures. Even with pedals that provide some amount of free rotation (or float), it's important to set your cleats properly.

The goal is to get your feet to automatically be in the center of the cleat's rotational arc, no matter what angle they assume naturally. This allows them to move a little on either side from your "neutral" center.

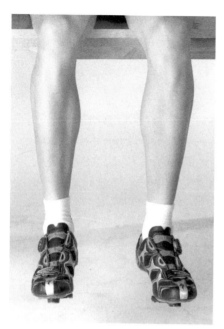

FIGURE 4.2 Sitting to determine natural foot position.

To find the correct angle to mount your cleats, sit on the edge of a table or counter and let your feet dangle. Keep your hips, knees, and ankles at 90-degree angles. Let your feet hang where they want to—don't force them to toe in or out. But do keep your ankles flexed at 90 degrees (see Figure 4.2).

Now look down to see the angles your feet are making. Those are the angles you should reproduce when you set your cleats. Have a friend help you by looking at your feet as they are dangling off the table and again when you mount the cleats and sit on the bike. But watch out: When some people bend forward, the angle of their feet changes due to internal rotation at the hips. So as you're checking the angles, bend forward on the table the same amount you do to reach the handlebar on your bike. If your foot angle changes, use the angle created when you lean forward.

Most people's feet don't toe in or out at the same angle. You will probably need to set each cleat at a different angle depending on how each foot behaves.

FOREFOOT VARUS

As many as 87 percent of all feet have forefoot varus, which means the ball of the foot is elevated in relation to the outside of the foot when the foot is not bearing weight.

In cycling, varus causes riders to internally rotate the shin as they put pressure on the pedal. This, in turn, drives the knee toward the top tube.

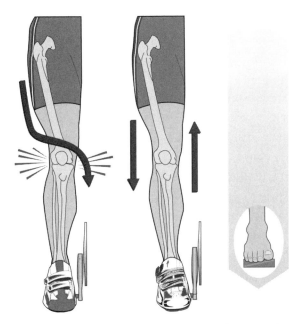

FIGURE 4.3 Uncorrected forefoot varus (left) can injure knees and steal pedaling power. The solution (right) is to use shoes, orthotics, or other devices that neutralize varus. *(Courtesy of Specialized)*

This results in a significant loss of power and is the most common cause of anterior medial knee injuries.

Forefoot varus can be neutralized by custom orthotics, wedges made by Bicycle Fitting Systems, Inc., or anatomic shoes such as the Body Geometry models from Specialized (see Figure 4.3). These alter the angle of the foot as it connects to the pedal, keeping it in a neutral position. As a result, the knee does not move in, and strain on the knee is reduced.

PEDAL FLOAT

The first clipless pedals to be made didn't have float—the ability to let the foot rotate a few degrees outward or inward as you pedal. The result of this rigidity was foot and knee injuries. Today, however, nearly all clipless pedals permit float.

Most cleats allow between 3 and 6 degrees of rotation before they snap free from the pedal. For most riders, this is enough. A small percentage of riders might need a pedal system that provides more than 9 degrees of rotation.

The less float your cleats have, the more power you can produce. With more float, your leg muscles have to work harder to stabilize your foot as it rotates on the pedal. Therefore, it's best to choose pedals with the least amount of float you need.

Some extremely duck-footed riders need pedals with more float, but only so they can achieve their normal foot posture on the pedal.

Of course, your anklebones shouldn't hit the crank arms and your heels shouldn't hit the chainstays. If they do, you need orthotic arch supports and/or forefoot varus correction. With old-fashioned straight crank arms, riders with unstable feet from gross pronation and external tibial rotation would bang their anklebones frequently, especially when trying to put out lots of power on short hills while seated. Modern crank arms that curve or angle away from narrow bottom brackets all but eliminate this problem.

PART II

REMEDIES FOR CYCLING INJURIES

CHAPTER 5

KNEES

IT SEEMS LIKE CYCLING SHOULD BE HARD ON THE KNEES. AT AN average cadence of 90 rpm, a rider churns out 5,400 pedal revolutions per hour or about 1.5 million pedal strokes in a 5,000-mile year.

Yet cycling is relatively benign for this complex joint because it's not a high-impact sport. There's no heel strike as there is in running. In fact, bike riding is the recommended activity for rehabilitation of most knee injuries. Even if you can't walk, run, or limp around the block on crutches, you can ride a bike.

This is because cycling isn't a full-weight-bearing activity. The pedals are always descending away from you, which means you're not putting excessive stress on your knees. Injured knees, knees that have been surgically repaired, and aging knees all want movement—and you want exercise. It all comes together on a bike.

Occasionally, however, cyclists' knees do become injured. After all, that's one hardworking joint! The good news is that most knee problems respond quickly to treatment. This chapter takes you through a list of common cycling-related knee injuries and tells you what to do about them. In most cases, core treatment consists of two key components:

- Icing
- Taking pain-relieving anti-inflammatory medication (NSAID)

HOW TO ICE INJURIES

In general for injuries where icing is appropriate, apply ice as many as three times a day for 15 to 20 minutes each time. I frequently recommend icing injuries in this book. Here's the proper way to do it:

- Fill a plastic zip-shut food storage bag with crushed ice or small ice cubes. Place a cloth (a washcloth works well) on the skin over the injury. Lay the ice bag on top and use an elastic bandage to hold it in place (see Figure 5.1). Don't fasten the bandage too tightly or it will increase the cold on your skin, which could cause damage.
- Keep the ice pack in place for 15 to 20 minutes, then remove it for about 40 minutes, and reapply. (The general rule: Ice for 15 to 20 minutes each hour.) Repeat the process up to three times a day.

> **TIP:** *Some injuries respond to focal icing—rubbing ice directly on the exact spot of the pain. Fill a small paper cup nearly full with water and put it in the freezer overnight. Once it is frozen, gently massage the afflicted area with the exposed end of the ice, like you're rubbing it with an ice cream cone. As the ice melts, peel away the paper cup to expose more ice (see Figure 5.2). Place a towel*

FIGURE 5.1 Using an ice bag.   FIGURE 5.2 Focal icing.

*under the injury to absorb the melting ice. Stop when your skin be-
gins to get numb. Several 5-minute sessions per hour up to three
times a day should provide plenty of therapy for your ailment without injuring your skin.*

Here's a related technique you can try for an inflamed tendon. First,
ice the area. Then perform cross-friction massage by rubbing across the
tendon fibers with your thumb for about 10 minutes (see Figure 5.3).
Then reapply ice. Cross-friction massage may make the pain worse in the
short term, but improvement will quickly follow.

EXAMPLE: *A member of the U.S. Cycling Team with a bad case of
patellar tendinitis was flying to South America for a stage race. He
didn't think he would be able to compete. I instructed him to perform icing and cross-friction massage on the plane. After two days
of travel and self-treatment, he was ready to race.*

FIGURE 5.3 Using the thumb to do a cross-friction massage of the
patellar tendon.

HOW TO USE A NSAID

Another frequent fix for cycling injuries is the use of a nonsteroidal anti-inflammatory drug (NSAID). Common trade names are Aleve, Motrin, and Advil.

> **CAUTION!** *Although NSAIDs are over-the-counter medications, their use can be dangerous. Please obey the manufacturer's directions. In particular, excessive doses combined with dehydration can lead to kidney problems in some individuals.*

When using NSAIDs, you need to be especially careful riding on a tour or in periods of heavy training when you might become chronically dehydrated. Be sure you drink plenty of water when you're taking NSAIDs. Additionally, these medications can be tough on your stomach lining, so reduce the risk by taking them with food.

PATELLAR TENDINITIS

Description

Tendinitis is inflammation of a tendon, usually a result of overuse. Overdoing an activity places too much stress on the tendon before it is strong enough, and the result is microscopic tears in the tendon. The tears heal and become microscopic scars. The tearing and scarring cause the tendon to enlarge, producing an increase in friction in the tendon as it moves. The result is pain.

Patellar tendinitis refers specifically to an inflammation of the patella, or kneecap (see Figure 5.4). It's surrounded by the tendon structure that connects the quadriceps muscle group in the thigh to the lower leg.

Symptoms

Symptoms of patellar tendinitis include pain in the front of the knee, below the patella, when you pedal or walk upstairs. The pain is usually stronger when you're descending stairs. You may also experience pain when you merely touch the tendon. There may be some swelling. The pain is usually centered on the lower tip (inferior pole) of the patella where it connects to the tendon.

The tendon might squeak like a rusty hinge when you bend your knee. This worrisome noise is called crepitus and means the tendon's normal lubrication is in short supply.

If the tendinitis is severe, localized swelling may occur. It will look like a little grape at the end of your patella.

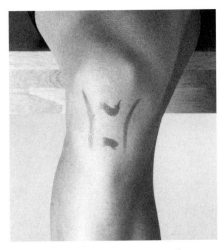

FIGURE 5.4 The location of patellar tendinitis.

Causes

This injury often appears after hard sprinting, climbing in a big gear, or off-bike jumping activities. It can also flare up after hard leg presses or squats. A combination of activities is often the culprit—riding hard early in the training season while also doing leg presses, for instance. A common cause is simply doing too much, too soon.

Treatment

- Apply ice to the knee as many as three times a day for 15 to 20 minutes each time.
- Take a nonsteroidal anti-inflammatory drug (NSAID) with food.
- Check the height of your saddle and make sure you've got the proper fit.
- Pedal easily or stop riding for several days.

SPRING KNEE

Description

This is another form of tendinitis that often strikes the complex of tendons in the front of the knee (see Figure 5.5). It's an injury that results from overuse and placing too much strain on a tendon that is too weak. It

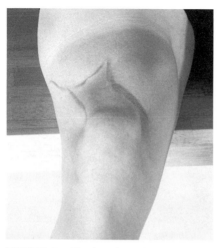

FIGURE 5.5 The location of spring knee shown on the right knee.

often starts in the early season, which gives it its name. But it's not just too many miles early in the season that cause this condition. It's typically the combination of riding, weight training, and other activities that enthusiastic cyclists do in the spring.

Symptoms

The main symptom of spring knee is a sharp pain along the top of the patella, which is a triangle-shaped bone with the single point at the bottom. The pain usually occurs on the inner (medial) or outer (lateral) points on top, though it can appear anywhere around the kneecap.

In rare cases, spring knee manifests itself as a tender spot two to three inches above the knee where tendon and muscle come together.

Causes

Spring knee is associated with a combination of activities that cyclists often do during the early season: leg exercises such as squats or leg presses, increased mileage on the bike, and perhaps downhill skiing—all in conjunction with cold weather that irritates tendons.

You are more likely to develop this injury when you are fit enough to work out hard, but your fitness activities are not cycling-specific.

Treatment

- Apply ice to the knee as many as three times a day for 15 to 20 minutes each time.
- Take a nonsteroidal anti-inflammatory drug (NSAID) with food.
- Check the height of your saddle and make sure you've got a proper fit.
- Pedal easily or stop riding for several days.

If Tendinitis Remedies Don't Work

If these remedies don't solve your problems with tendinitis, find the error in your training or position that led to the injury. If you rode too few miles before a long tour or hard ride, don't make the mistake again. Revise your training plan so you build your mileage gradually.

The problem may also be caused by a poor bike fit. Incorrect cleat position or saddle height can hurt knees. Refer to the fitting instructions in Chapters 2 and 4. If you're still having trouble, get a professional bike fit from a certified coach, a reputable bike shop, or a cycling-savvy facility such as the Boulder Center for Sports Medicine.

If pain persists, it can be treated with cortisone to reduce the inflammation. A physical therapist can use phonophoresis, which delivers cortisone cream into the afflicted area using ultrasound. Injected cortisone is definitely *not* recommended due to possible long-term complications.

Returning to Riding after Tendinitis

When tendinitis pain has eased, there are a few things you can do to avoid another flare-up.

- Before riding, apply a counterirritant to increase blood flow to the area. Use a commercial product (such as Icy Hot) or make your own by mixing baby oil and oil of wintergreen.
- Shield the injured knee from cool wind with leg warmers or a light coating of petroleum jelly.
- Increase your cadence and reduce pedaling resistance by using lower gears.
- Raise your saddle about 3 mm, and always wear leg warmers or tights if the temperature is below 65°F.

CHONDROMALACIA

Description

Chondromalacia is the softening and degeneration of articular cartilage on the back of the patella (kneecap). It can range from an irritation to actual degeneration that can lead to arthritis. It can also be accompanied by other inflammatory conditions like tendinitis or bursitis. Chondromalacia (and its associated inflammations) is the most common complaint in cycling.

However, the term is often used to mean any patellar discomfort. It's a "garbage can" term for sore knees in general. Other terms often used interchangeably are "extensor mechanism dysfunction," "patellar femoral pain syndrome," or simply "overuse."

Symptoms

The most obvious symptom of chondromalacia is pain behind the patella that often occurs when you're climbing or descending stairs or pushing big gears.

There might also be audible clicking or grating, and you may experience aching and stiffness after sitting.

Causes

Chondromalacia is caused by overuse or trauma on the kneecap. This could be from too much kneeling or squatting, excessive use of big gears and a slow cadence, or weight training activities, such as leg extensions, that isolate and load the patella.

It could also be caused by an abnormal alignment of the patella. The cartilage on the back of the kneecap can be roughened until it loses its normal glossy surface, resulting in irritation and pain. Like the tires on a car that's out of alignment, the kneecap can wear unevenly.

Treatment

Cycling is generally good for chondromalacia because knees like smooth circles. Your saddle should be set high—the lower the saddle, the more shearing force on the back of the kneecap. Raise the saddle until your hips begin rocking during the pedal stroke, then lower it just enough to stop this motion.

> **TIP:** Any time you raise the saddle, also raise the stem the same amount. This way, you'll retain your ideal differential between the height of the handlebar and the top of the saddle.

Additionally, to treat chondromalacia:

- Apply ice as many as three times a day for 15 to 20 minutes each time.
- Take a nonsteroidal anti-inflammatory drug (NSAID) with food.
- Ride with a high cadence and low gears so there's little resistance on each pedal stroke. Avoid climbing, especially in the saddle.

If These Remedies Don't Work

Chondromalacia treatment has become a real art. See a therapist if the above remedies don't improve your condition. A therapist will likely follow the McConnell theory of strengthening the vastus medialis (the pear-shaped part of the quadriceps muscle just above and to the inner side of your knee). This theory is named after an Australian physical therapist who pioneered the use of stretching exercises and taping techniques to remedy chondromalacia. There are multiple theories of treatment, but McConnell's is well known and quite effective. (In fact, one way to check the qualifications of any physical therapist you're considering to provide treatment is to ask if they use the McConnell method. They may prefer another approach, but if they're ignorant of McConnell, you should look elsewhere.)

Your therapist should prescribe short-arc leg extensions and straight-leg raises, as well as cycling. Some therapists tape the patella and surrounding area, although this is a temporary treatment.

Long-term relief from chondromalacia comes from developing a high level of vastus medialis strength combined with gluteal (butt muscle) strength. (See Chapter 19 for specific exercises.)

When chondromalacia sufferers can walk downstairs pain-free after therapy, they usually have the symptoms under control.

ILIOTIBIAL BAND FRICTION SYNDROME

Description

The iliotibial (IT) band is a wide sheath of fibrous connective tissue that extends from the crest of the hipbone to slightly below the knee along the outer side of the thigh (see Figure 5.6).

The IT band's lower end crosses the bony protuberance on the outer side of the knee. There is a bursa (fluid-filled sack) located between the bone and the IT band that provides protection and lubrication. In some situations, this area can be irritated. IT band friction syndrome is not only an inflammation of the tissue, it's also bursitis.

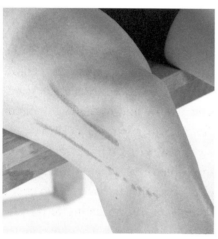

FIGURE 5.6 IT band location on the right knee.

Symptoms

The symptom of IT band friction syndrome is a sharp, stabbing pain on the outside, middle of the knee. It usually begins as a mild twinge, then increases until it feels like someone is tightening a hose clamp or stabbing you with a screwdriver. Maximum friction occurs between the midpoint of the stroke and the bottom dead center, which means the pain is usually worse during the power portion of the pedal stroke.

Causes

Problems with the IT band can be caused by poor bike fit: a stance on the bike that's too narrow, badly positioned cleats (usually they're too toed-in, but this isn't always the case), a saddle that is too high, or pedals that don't allow float. Biomechanical factors such as "bowlegs" or flat feet can also contribute to the problem.

Additionally, too much riding too soon can cause this problem. IT problems rarely happen after a period of base mileage.

Treatment

To solve the immediate problem, apply ice as many as three times a day for 10 to 15 minutes each time, and take a nonsteroidal anti-inflammatory drug (NSAID) with food.

Additionally, you may need to make some changes to your bike fit. Widen your stance on the bike by moving your cleats as far to the inside of the shoe sole as possible. Or put a washer on the pedal axle to prevent the pedal from threading as far into the crank arm. (Use a washer that's no more than 2 mm thick so enough pedal screws in to be safe.) Some road riders install a triple crankset, or one with a third chainring, on their bikes to take advantage of the longer bottom bracket axle to widen their stance.

If your pedals don't have "float," it may help to position your cleats so your feet angle more than normal. This should be a very slight adjustment that puts your heel fractionally closer to the crank arm when pedaling.

Also, lower your saddle about 6 mm. (IT band friction syndrome is one of the few knee problems in which the saddle should be lowered rather than raised.)

Over-the-counter arch supports or custom orthotics are often helpful because controlling the arch controls excessive tibial (lower leg) rotation. For this reason, anatomic shoes, such as the Body Geometry models by Specialized, are effective.

> **CAUTION!** *If these treatments don't relieve the pain in one day, stop riding but continue icing and NSAIDs. Once IT band friction syndrome gets established, it's hard to correct.*

If These Remedies Don't Work

If these remedies don't solve the problem, you need to do specific stretches, such as the OBER stretch, on a regular basis. Learn them from a qualified physical therapist (see Figure 5.7).

You can also consider localized cortisone injections for temporary relief to stop the inflammation. However, cortisone is indicated only when the tendons to be injected aren't under a constant load. Cortisone tends to "dry out" the tissue, causing necrosis (tissue damage). This can lead to a ruptured tendon.

In persistent cases, a relatively simple surgical procedure can save the day. A surgeon removes a small section of the afflicted IT band, eliminating the pain.

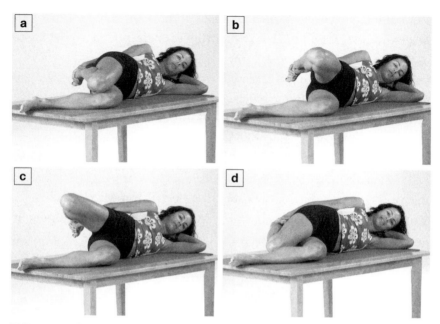

FIGURE 5.7 Performing the OBER stretch for IT band friction syndrome.

PLICA SYNDROME

Description

A plica is a piece of synovial tissue (lining of the joint) that becomes inflamed. During development in the embryo, the knee is originally divided into three compartments, which later develop into one larger compartment. In about 70 percent of humans, the membranes that divided these compartments do not completely disappear. Pain occurs when this tissue becomes trapped between the patella (kneecap) and the femur (thighbone).

Symptoms

Plica syndrome (see Figure 5.8) begins as an ache. Most medical professionals initially mistake it for chondromalacia. Eventually it becomes a sharp pain on the medial (inner) side of the knee in the crease beside the patella. It feels like something is being sawed against the sharp, bony edges of the patella and femur. In rare cases, the pain is felt in other parts of the knee.

Causes

Plica syndrome often accompanies a saddle that's set too low. Additionally, knock-knees and flat feet put stress on the connective tissue on the inside of the knee, pulling the plica tight like a string.

Overuse is often a factor.

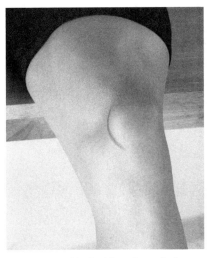

FIGURE 5.8 Typical location of plica syndrome pain.

Treatment

- Rest off the bike.
- Apply ice to the knee as many as three times a day for 15 to 20 minutes each time.
- Take a nonsteroidal antiinflammatory drug (NSAID).
- Change activities, perhaps substituting fast walking for cycling. Modify your activities until you can ride pain-free. A good way to test this is to spin gently on an indoor trainer. If pain returns, you can simply get off the trainer. If you were riding outside, you might have to pedal all the way home with a suddenly painful knee, which could set back your treatment.

If These Remedies Don't Work

Because the plica is often irritated by a saddle that's too low, raising the saddle about 3 mm can often reduce the symptoms. Persistent plica pain that lasts a year or longer can be stopped by surgical removal of the offending tissue.

INFLAMMATION OF THE MEDIAL PATELLAR FEMORAL LIGAMENT

Description

The medial patellar femoral ligament (MPFL) (see Figure 5.9) is a band of tissue running from the inner border of the kneecap to the thighbone.

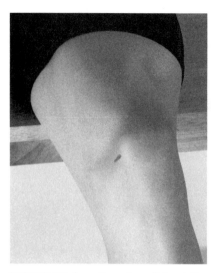

FIGURE 5.9 Location of medial patellar femoral ligament.

Only about 70 percent of the population has an identifiable MPFL. It rarely becomes inflamed except in repetitive sports like cycling.

Symptoms

The symptom of MPFL inflammation is a sharp pain on the medial (inner) side of the knee. It can be isolated to a pinpoint pain on the inner edge of the kneecap.

Causes

Causes include a saddle that's too low and pedals that have too much float, which cause the MPFL to work harder to control the kneecap if there's too much tibial rotation. Knock-knees, flat feet, or tight iliotibial bands can also cause MPFL inflammation.

Treatment

- Apply ice directly to the spot of pain as many as three times a day for 15 to 20 minutes each time.
- Rest off the bike.
- Get a cortisone injection, which sometimes helps.
- Have your bike fit by a professional if you are knock-kneed or flat-footed. Orthotics or forefoot varus wedging may also help.
- Avoid pedals that allow excessive float.

If These Remedies Don't Work

In advanced and persistent cases, steroid injections can be used after six months of trying the less-aggressive treatments listed above.

If steroid injections don't produce improvement in an additional six months, this condition can be treated with a surgical release of the ligament.

PES ANSERINE BURSITIS/TENDINITIS

Description

Pes anserine is Latin for "goose-foot," a description of what the three medial hamstrings (tendons located on the inner side of the knee) look like in a dissected cadaver where they connect to the medial flare of the tibia. Aren't you glad you asked?

These tendons can become inflamed and cause pain. Another possible cause of pain is inflammation of the bursa that underlies the tendons. A bursa is a small sac of fluid that sits between the tendons and the bone. It's difficult to dis-

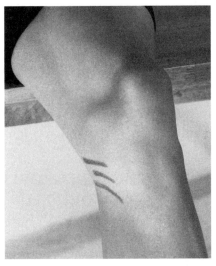

FIGURE 5.10 Location of pain from pes anserine bursitis/tendinitis in left knee.

tinguish between inflammation of the tendons and inflammation of the bursa, but the treatment for both conditions is the same.

Symptoms

The symptoms of pes anserine bursitis/tendinitis (see Figure 5.10) are sharp pain on the medial portion of the knee about one inch below its center, and swelling, tenderness, and pain when you touch or stretch the area.

Causes

Improper bike fit is one possible cause. This includes an excessively high saddle, a pedal system with too much float, and a stance on the pedals that is too wide.

Riding a fixed-gear (track) bike can also cause this, as can knock-knees or flat feet.

Treatment

- Lower the saddle about 3 mm.

- Apply ice as many as three times a day for 15 to 20 minutes each time.
- Take a nonsteroidal anti-inflammatory drug (NSAID) with food.

If These Remedies Don't Work

If you're still having problems, get fitted for a good cycling orthotic. Additionally, switch to pedals with less float (less than 8 degrees of rotation to each side of neutral). Pedals that allow generous foot rotation make the problem worse because the pes anserine has to work hard to stabilize the tibial (lower leg) rotation that results.

BICEPS FEMORIS TENDINITIS OR POPLITEUS TENDINITIS

Description

The biceps femoris is the hamstring that attaches to the outer side of the knee on the back of the fibula (lower leg). Tendinitis here is often confused with IT band syndrome, but with tendinitis, the pain is lower down the outside of the knee (see Figure 5.11).

Pain in the same area may also involve the popliteus, a muscle smaller than your little finger. It attaches in the same general area as the biceps femoris and controls the rotation of the tibia. Both conditions are treated the same way.

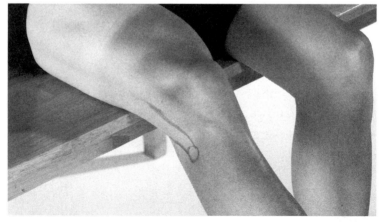

FIGURE 5.11 Location of biceps femoris or popliteus tendinitis in left knee.

Symptoms

The symptom of either of these types of tendinitis is pain on the outer side of the knee about one inch below the middle of the joint and slightly above the bony protuberance.

Causes

It can be caused by a saddle that's too high or by riding a fixed-gear (track) bike. While riding a fixed gear, the hamstrings are used to decelerate, putting them under load and sometimes irritating the biceps femoris tendon.

Bow-legged people often suffer from this problem as well.

Pedals with excessive float make the problem worse because the biceps femoris and popliteal tendons have to work hard to stabilize the excessive tibial rotation that results.

Treatment

- Apply ice as many as three times a day for 15 to 20 minutes each time.
- Take a nonsteroidal anti-inflammatory drug (NSAID) with food.
- Lower the saddle about 3 mm.
- Switch to a pedal system with limited or no float.

If These Remedies Don't Work

Because biceps femoris tendinitis is often caused by riding a fixed-gear (track) bike, changing to a bike with a freewheel often alleviates the problem.

FREQUENTLY ASKED QUESTIONS: KNEES

Q: How should I care for knees on rides?

There are several things you can do to take care of your knees while you ride.

Keep your knees warm. Riding in chilly temperatures with bare knees is a recipe for trouble. The knee's tendons lie exposed near the skin's surface. My rule is to cover your knees with leg warmers or tights if the air temperature is below 65°F.

Warm up. Your knees need at least fifteen minutes of gradual spinning to get the blood flowing. Start in a small gear and gradually increase both the resistance and the cadence until you're sweating lightly and your knees feel loose. Blasting out of your driveway in the big ring and attacking the first hill can lead to disaster.

Spin. Keep your cadence between 80 and 110 rpm on the flats and no lower than 70 rpm when you're climbing in the saddle. If you're standing while climbing, you can go a bit lower, but not much. Low cadences and big gears are an unholy alliance, putting major strain on knee tendons. Look at the pros—they spin at high cadences with a pedal stroke that's silky smooth.

Build mileage gradually. The standard recommendation is to increase mileage no more than 10 percent from one week to the next. You need to let your knees adapt to the workload.

Change with caution. You knees are creatures of habit. They don't like new strains or stresses. If you've been riding on flat roads all season, work into climbing gradually. If you decide to install longer crank arms, don't ride 100 miles the first time out on the new equipment. Easy does it.

Q: What if I have a preexisting knee injury?

Sometimes, a person's bike fits fine and he undertakes a smart, gradual, and moderate training program. But his knee hurts anyway. In this case, suspect a preexisting injury that has flared up from cycling.

For example, you may have suffered a slight cartilage tear in another sport, such as football. Cycling is great for this sort of chronic knee problem, so reduce mileage and continue to ride. Your body should soon adapt. If it doesn't and you continue to experience pain, see an orthopedist or physical therapist.

Q: What are custom cycling orthotics, and do I need them?

Orthotics are supports used inside shoes. They are a great way to correct the "imperfections" in the biomechanics of your feet. They are custom-made to fit your unique feet, so they offer support that is far superior to generic insoles or footbeds.

Most orthotics are meant for walking or running. Therefore, they are "heel posted," meaning that they are designed for a stride where the heel hits first. They are also relatively short, extending from heel to just behind the ball of the foot. But in cycling, it's not the heel but the ball of the foot that makes contact with the pedal. As a result, cycling orthotics are "forefoot posted." They extend beyond the arch nearly to the toes.

Do you need custom orthotics for cycling? Consider using orthotics if your ankles pronate (or tilt inward) badly, if you have flat feet, or if you experience persistent knee pain that proper bike fit and other healthy-knee measures in this book don't cure.

Have your orthotics made by a cycling-knowledgeable podiatrist, physical therapist, or athletic trainer.

Q: How can I keep my knees healthy off the bike?

Don't squat or kneel excessively. Squatting puts excessive pressure on the back of the kneecap, while kneeling pushes the kneecap into the bony groove of the femur (thighbone). This can cause damage.

Don't climb or descend hills or stairs. Walking down exposes any weaknesses you have in muscle groups such as your quadriceps' vastus medialis. Running downhill is especially hard on knees. Mountain runners are used to the pounding of hard descents on rubbly trails, but they've trained long and hard to accustom their knees to the abuse.

Don't do weight exercises that isolate the kneecap. These include full-range leg extensions and full squats. These exercises cause compressing and shearing forces on the back of the kneecap. When doing leg extensions, limit movement to the final 25 degrees before your knees straighten. On squats and leg presses, don't bend your knees more than 90 degrees.

If you do everything right and your knees still hurt, seek an expert's help.

CHAPTER 6

BACK AND NECK

Low back pain is the second most common complaint of cyclists. (Knee pain is the first.) And the frequency is rising as the population ages.

Among the general population, low back pain afflicts 80 percent of adults. About 10 million people miss work each day because of it. It doesn't seem to matter whether a person is a sedentary desk jockey or a manual laborer—back pain affects everyone equally.

Fortunately, about 40 percent of sufferers get better in one week, and almost 90 percent get better in a month, even without specific treatment. But 90 percent of people who experience low back pain one time are doomed to have recurring episodes. What's worse, with each episode, recovery time lengthens.

BACK PAIN

Description
There are many causes of low back pain among the general population, ranging from weak core muscles to nerve damage to aging disks. But for cyclists, the causes are fairly simple: They usually boil down to improper bike fit or poor riding position. If you have an existing low back problem, poor bike fit can make it even worse.

Neck pain is less prevalent in cyclists. But it can be a real plague, especially among long-distance cyclists who hold their heads in the riding position for hours or days at a time. Time trialists and triathletes are likely sufferers, too, because they get so low on the bike that they have to crane their necks to see ahead. This puts extra stress on the joints of the cervical spine.

Symptoms

Symptoms of back pain include experiencing sharp pain in the muscles along the spine or a dull ache in the area just above the pelvis. Sharp pain between the shoulder blades is a symptom of upper back pain.

Causes

According to laboratory studies, the most common cause of back pain in cyclists is a leg length inequality, either structural or functional. A structural inequality means that the legs are of different length due to actual inequalities in bone length. But leg length inequalities can also be functional, resulting from severe pronation in one foot that causes the arch to collapse, a degenerative knee, or a rotated pelvis.

Incorrect bike fit is a frequent contributor, especially too much reach to the handlebar, which leads to muscle fatigue and spasms. Lack of "core" strength in the torso can cause fatigue and back pain.

Back pain may plague cyclists who attempt mileage significantly greater than they are used to riding.

Additionally, biomechanical low back pain might result from degenerative disk disease, lordosis (swayback), scoliosis (lateral curvature of the spine), or age-related wear and tear.

Upper back pain has a list of diagnoses similar to low back pain. Included are degenerative disk disease, kyphosis (humpback), scoliosis, age-related wear and tear, muscle weakness, and muscle spasms due to poor bike fit.

Treatment

Applying ice and taking anti-inflammatory medication often helps with the pain. Additionally, a commercial bandage impregnated with a counterirritant ("hot stuff") often provides some relief, probably because you feel the heat of the wintergreen rather than the back pain.

To treat back pain, you'll need to make some changes to the fit of your bike. Raise the handlebars to put yourself in a higher riding position. This will reduce strain on the low back by reducing how far forward you have to bend.

> **CAUTION!** *When raising the handlebar, never exceed the maximum height line that's etched into the stem. If you do, the stem could break off during a ride. You will need more than this book to remedy what happens after that.*

If your reach to the handlebar is excessive, a higher stem may alleviate the problem even if it's the same length. A bike's head tube is slanted to the rear, so raising the stem also shortens the reach.

If you have a conventional stem, pull it farther out of the steerer tube to raise the handlebar. You can also get a higher position by loosening the stem's binder bolt to rotate the handlebar upward slightly, raising the brake levers.

On bikes with threadless headsets and stems, adjustment usually requires buying a new stem with more rise (upward angle). Some stems are reversible and provide more rise if they're turned over, so check this first before you replace the stem entirely.

However, some forks that are designed for threadless headsets have a carbon steerer tube. It's dangerous to extend a carbon steerer tube too far above the head tube. Use no more than about 4 cm of spacers to raise the bars. Check the specifications from your fork manufacturer for specific recommendations.

Get a professional bike fit by a qualified coach, trainer, or shop employee. Remember that there's a big difference between a coach's fit, which is performance based, and a bike shop's fit, which is comfort based. Be sure you know what you need for meeting your goals in the sport. If back pain is a problem, it's better to get a bike fit from a medical professional who is better qualified to take into consideration the medical ramifications of low back problems.

If stem and position adjustments don't work, you may need a bike with a shorter top tube. Get the advice of a qualified professional (or two) before making this major investment.

Practice good riding habits. Move around on the bike to take pressure off your back. Change hand positions and stand up for one minute in every five, even if the terrain doesn't encourage it. On long seated climbs, slide to the back of the saddle, to the middle, and then to the front.

If These Remedies Don't Work

If you've got the proper bike fit and you're practicing good riding habits but you're still experiencing back pain, it is possible that you have a leg length inequality (LLI). There are two ways to check this:

1. The simplest method is a *standing AP pelvis*, an X-ray of your hip region taken from the front while you're standing. The technician can then measure the difference in the height of your femoral heads to determine your functional leg length inequality. This doesn't, however, tell in which leg segments an inequality exists. The technician will have to judge this, and it's an inaccurate science that takes considerable expertise.
2. LLI also can be determined from a *scanogram* X-ray, although this can be difficult for an inexperienced technician. In a scanogram, your leg bones are measured by including a meter stick in the X-ray image.

Scanograms are rarely needed anymore. A standing AP pelvis and a good clinical exam are usually enough for an experienced specialist to find the location of the leg length inequality. LLIs of as little as 3 mm can be enough to cause back pain in some riders, especially those doing high mileage or who have a history of low back pain. The solution is to shim the cleat or shift the foot in relation to the pedal (described in the next section).

Additionally, strengthen your abs and low back musculature by doing crunches and partial back extensions, and increase lower back flexibility with appropriate stretches. A physical therapist can teach you several effective ones.

TIP: *See a qualified physical therapist to get an exercise and stretching regimen designed for you. You'll need the correct diagnosis of your problem to get the best results.*

FREQUENTLY ASKED QUESTIONS: SHIMMING CLEATS

Q: When should I shim a cleat?

If you have a leg length inequality (LLI) of 3 mm or greater accompanied by back pain, you may need a shim. For walking or running, most orthopedists won't adjust for an LLI until the difference between legs is 6 mm or more.

In cycling, if the LLI is less than 6 mm, I don't use a shim. Instead, I move the cleat on the side with the short leg forward on the shoe sole 1 to 2 mm. You can move the cleat on the foot on the long leg backward to get the same effect. Rarely do you have to compensate for the full amount of the LLI. These techniques have the effect of making the foot on the short leg slightly longer to compensate for the difference in leg length.

If the LLI is over 6 mm, it requires a shim.

Q: How do I shim my cleat?

The shim should be placed between the shoe sole and the cleat (see Figure 6.1). Look and Look-compatible road cleats are the easiest to shim, while Shimano SPD cleats (both road and off-road) are slightly harder. Other brands vary from fairly easy to difficult. Several makes of high-end road cleats are impossible to shim.

Shoe repair and prosthetic-device shops can shim your cleats if you explain what you want. You can also do it yourself. Here's how:

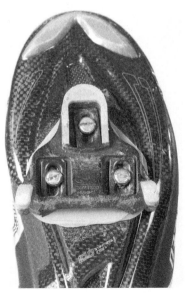

FIGURE 6.1 Shoe sole and cleat showing placement of shim.

FIGURE 6.2 Note the shim between the cleat and the shoe sole.

1. Choose a material to use as a shim. Neolite, available in shoe repair shops, works well for Look road cleats. Fairly hard plastic or aluminum bar stock is often used for Shimano SPD cleats. Choose a material that is hard enough to resist compression but soft enough for the serrated bottom of the cleat to make an impression: The cleat should not be able to slide when the bolts are tightened or when it's entering or exiting the pedal.

2. Cut the shim so the thickness is about half the amount of your leg length inequality. This is as long as it needs to be. Your body has already adjusted for much of the LLI via various physical compensations; adjusting for the entire amount would be overkill. So if your LLI is 8 mm, make the shim 3 to 4 mm thick.

3. Obtain longer bolts to accommodate the added thickness of the shim. Take one of the stock bolts to a hardware store to use as a basis for measuring.

4. Cut the shim material in the shape of the cleat.

5. Drill bolt holes.

6. Align the bolt holes, and glue the shim to the sole of the shoe. Hold it with a C-clamp until it's dry. If you have the three-hole Campagnolo cleat, make sure the shim does not protrude outside the cleat or it won't engage properly.

7. Reattach the cleat.

8. On shoes with recessed cleat pockets, the shimmed cleat will protrude beyond the sole, causing it to touch the ground when you
walk. If this bothers you, build up the sole around the cleat with
Shoe Goo, a product for repairing running shoe soles. It's available
in shoe repair shops or sporting goods stores.

Q: My scanogram X-ray showed a leg length discrepancy of 8 mm.
Most of it is in my femur rather than in my lower leg. Does this
change how I shim my cleat?

A femoral LLI is hard to correct. When one thighbone is shorter than the
other, you can't sit square on the saddle. The center of the knee should
be directly over the pedal axle, and that's impossible when the upper legs
are of different lengths. Riders with this problem can't get completely
comfortable on the bike no matter what they do.

The solution is to shim and move the cleat on the short leg. For example,
with an 8 mm LLI in which most of the difference is femoral, I'd shim
the cleat 3 mm and move the cleat on the short leg forward on the shoe sole
about 2 mm. (Remember that you don't compensate for the full amount, so
this doesn't add up to 8 mm.) Sliding the cleat forward has the effect of
lengthening the foot and leg, helping to center that knee over the pedal.

SHERMER NECK

Description

Shermer neck is named after Michael Shermer, a Race Across America
(RAAM) competitor who suffered from what can be termed neck failure.
Things got so bad that his crew members constructed a makeshift brace
from bungee cords to hold up his head as he rode. Shermer isn't the only
RAAM rider to suffer debilitating neck fatigue and pain, but he was the
first and, now, most famous.

Debilitating neck pain afflicts even the most well-conditioned long-
distance cyclists. The winner of the 2003 RAAM, Allen Larsen, had suffered so much in his initial attempt at the race in 2002 that his crew
came prepared in 2003 with a custom-designed neck brace to hold up his
head when his muscles were no longer up to the task.

Symptoms

Symptoms of Shermer neck include a tightness and pain in your neck after you've been riding a while. It's hard to turn your head to the side or look behind for traffic. In extreme cases, such as riding 350 miles day after day in the Race Across America, the neck muscles go into spasm. Like Shermer, riders can no longer hold up their head.

Causes

Shermer neck can be caused by improper bike fit, primarily excessive reach to the handlebar that makes you crane your neck to see ahead. Riding in an aerodynamic position that requires you to hyperextend your neck to see down the road can also strain the neck.

Insufficient strength in the neck muscles and riding long distances without taking sufficient breaks are also causes.

Treatment

- Raise your stem, or install a shorter, high-rise stem.
- If you're using aero bars, raise them so you can look ahead without straining your neck.
- Change position frequently as you ride. Stand often so your neck is supported by your spine rather than your muscles. Frequently turn your head from side to side and up and down to stretch and relax your neck.
- Tilt your head slightly to the left or right of vertical, rather than locking it into the dead center position.

If These Remedies Don't Work

If these fixes don't work and you're still experiencing neck pain, strengthen your neck muscles. See a physical therapist or ask your cycling coach for recommended exercises.

When you ride, increase your mileage gradually so your neck has a chance to become conditioned to holding your head in the riding position for longer periods.

CHAPTER 7

FOOT AND ANKLE

IT'S GENERALLY AGREED THAT FOOT PAIN CAN BE THE MOST agonizing in our sport. Foot pain can make cycling unbearable. Greg LeMond, three-time Tour de France winner, was a famous sufferer and needed custom shoes to alleviate his misery. But with modern anatomical shoes as well as custom cycling orthotics, there's no reason you have to suffer the agony of "de feet."

In an attempt to develop better cycling shoes, I teamed with Specialized Bicycle Components, Inc., in 2000 to design the Body Geometry shoe line. The technical features of these shoes include a longitudinal arch support, forefoot varus wedge as part of the outsole, and an arch cushion and a metatarsal arch support as part of the sock liner. Body Geometry shoes should reduce the need for custom orthotics in up to 90 percent of cyclists. However, not everyone needs special shoes to relieve foot pain; try the remedies here first to address your problems.

HOT FOOT

Description
Cyclists use the general term "hot foot" to describe a number of foot discomforts that produce the sensation of heat as well as pain.

Symptoms

Symptoms of hot foot include numb toes, pain under the ball of the foot, and the sensation that someone is searing the bottom of your foot with a blowtorch.

Causes

These unpleasant symptoms (called metatarsalgia) are generally caused by nerves squeezed between the metatarsal heads (foot bones) in the ball of the foot just behind the toes. A Morton's neuroma, in contrast, is a specific inflamed nerve between the third and fourth metatarsal spaces.

Tight shoes are often the culprit. Leather cycling shoes, common fifteen years ago, stretched with use to give feet room. But today's synthetic uppers don't stretch much. If shoes are tight when you buy them, they will remain tight and are likely to cause problems, especially on long rides. Additionally, most cycling shoes are simply a flat-bottom box for your feet. But most feet aren't flat. Cyclists need anatomical footbeds or orthotics to support their feet in these badly designed shoes.

The feet themselves can sometimes be the cause of hot foot. Unsupported forefoot varus (an abnormal degree of bend in the foot) often causes hot foot. Some narrow, bony, thin feet are extremely susceptible to hot foot because they lack padding. Fat, meaty, wide feet are at high risk, too, because they're often jammed into cycling shoes that are too narrow. Additionally, feet can become bruised on the sole by hard pedaling or lengthy climbs.

Another source of the problem could be small pedals. A small pedal concentrates pressure on one part of the foot instead of spreading pressure like a large-platform pedal. This generally isn't a problem with high-quality road shoes because their rigid sole distributes the pressure. But shoes with flexible soles—including most mountain bike shoes suitable for walking—usually compress the points where the pedal contacts the sole, passing the pressure on the foot.

Treatment

Treating hot foot requires redistributing the weight of your feet on the pedal to avoid putting pressure on a concentrated section of nerves in the balls of your feet. To redistribute pressure on your feet, move your cleats back about 2 mm and lower your saddle the same amount. You should feel significant improvement. To make more room in tight shoes, install thinner insoles or use thinner cycling socks. This can be a quick fix if you're on a tour and in pain.

Orthotics or shoe inserts with a metatarsal bump often help. A metatarsal bump is a small domed area in the footbed just behind the ball of the foot (see Figure 7.1). The bump spreads the bones of the forefoot, taking pressure off the nerves between them.

Some riders have good luck with so-called metatarsal arch buttons. You stick these small foam buttons to the insole just behind the ball of the foot. They work like the metatarsal bump in orthotics. Find these buttons in the foot-care section of a drugstore, or make your own from dense foam.

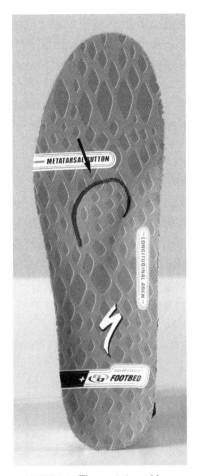

FIGURE 7.1 The metatarsal bump in a footbed.

If These Remedies Don't Work

If these don't work, purchase pedals with a larger platform. Additionally, plastic wedges, such as Bicycle Fitting System's bio-wedges, can be placed between the cleat and the sole of the shoe to level the foot on the pedal and distribute pressure.

Different shoes can also help. Buy shoes with a wider toe box, a stiffer sole, and an anatomical footbed. At the time of this writing, Specialized Body Geometry shoes are the best example.

Doctors may treat Morton's neuroma with cortisone injections. In advanced cases, if several cortisone injections fail, surgery is indicated.

Long-distance cyclists, especially those competing in grueling events like the Furnace Creek 508, Paris-Brest-Paris, or the Race Across America, often choose to wear their cleats so far behind the ball of the foot that they have to drill new holes in the sole. This is an extreme measure that should not be undertaken unless hot foot persists after you've exhausted all other remedies.

ACHILLES TENDINITIS

Description
Achilles tendinitis is an inflammation of the Achilles tendon on the back of the ankle, between where the tendon attaches to the heel bone and where it merges with the calf muscle.

Symptoms
The main symptom of Achilles tendinitis is pain in the tendon. There may also be an area of swelling that looks like a small grape on the tendon. In some cases, the tendon squeaks like a rusty hinge when you move the foot up and down by bending the ankle.

Causes
Achilles tendinitis can be caused by simple overuse. Increasing your mileage too quickly or doing lots of climbing when you aren't accustomed to it can inflame the tendon. Additionally, having the cleat positioned too far forward so you are pedaling "on your toes" causes excessive use of the calf muscle during the pedal stroke.

Faulty foot mechanics, such as excessive pronation (inward tilting of the ankle), or a tight Achilles tendon are also causes.

Treatment
For immediate relief, it's best to rest off the bike, apply ice up to three times per day for 10 to 15 minutes each time, and take a nonsteroidal anti-inflammatory drug (NSAID) with food.

To reduce strain on the Achilles when you ride, move your foot forward on the pedal by moving the cleat toward the heel of the shoe. Then

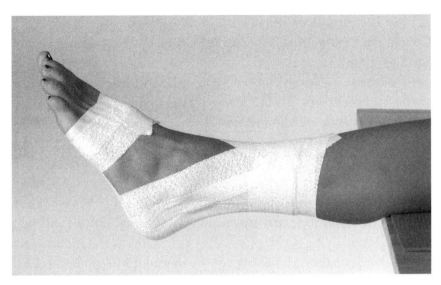

FIGURE 7.2 Taping of the Achilles tendon.

lower the saddle an amount equal to the distance you moved the cleats. Keep your body symmetrical by moving both cleats and treating both ankles equally, even though only one may be giving you a problem.

If you must keep riding on a tour, tape the ankle to lessen movement and reduce stress on the tendon (see Figure 7.2).

> **TIP:** *To tape your ankle for Achilles tendon relief, point your toe down about 30 degrees and run a prestretched strip of 3-inch elastic tape from the ball of the foot to the heel, then up the Achilles to the middle of the calf. Hold the bandage in place with tape applied like you'd normally tape an ankle for stability. The idea is to immobilize the ankle so much that you can't dorsiflex it (bring your toes toward your shin) while you pedal. This lessens strain on the Achilles.*

Stretch a tight Achilles tendon by standing 2 to 3 feet from a wall or tree. Extend your arms and lean in by bending your elbows while keeping your heels on the ground. Check with a physical therapist for other stretching exercises.

If These Remedies Don't Work

Custom cycling orthotics often help Achilles tendinitis by correcting angulation of the rear foot.

In some cases, an excessive amount of pedal float irritates the Achilles tendon because it has to work hard to stabilize the foot on the pedal. Switching to pedals with limited float may offer relief.

ANKLING—USEFUL OR NOT?

Ankling is pedaling with the toes pointing down at the bottom of the stroke to help pull the pedal around using the strength of the calf (see Figure 7.3).

This once-popular technique is now outmoded. EMG studies, a diagnostic tool used to measure the electrical activity of muscles, have shown that calves are poor power producers in cycling. Most of the power in the pedal stroke is generated by the quadriceps of the thigh and the glutes of the butt. The calves are merely the cables that transfer the power of the

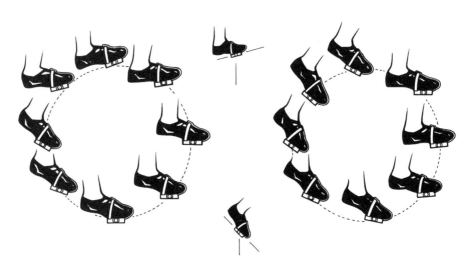

FIGURE 7.3 A relatively natural pedal stroke is shown at left. The illustration at right shows an attempt to "ankle" and bring the calf muscles into play. *(Adapted from* Science of Cycling*)*

quads to your foot and the pedal. Therefore, ankling will not result in any more power and may actually be a waste of energy.

Some people ankle modestly by nature, but 3-D studies of pedal strokes reveal that the total ankle bend is typically 10 degrees or less. It's incredibly small. Ankling is most likely an adjustment for the location of the tibial shaft in the pedal stroke. As your foot comes over the top, you drop your heel slightly. As you approach the bottom of the stroke, you point your toe down slightly.

Don't think consciously about ankling. Instead, try to apply pressure to the pedal all the way around the stroke. Greg LeMond's advice is still on target: Pull your foot through the bottom of the pedal stroke by imagining that you're scraping mud off your shoe. The next thing you know, your foot will be back at the top. (LeMond, incidentally, was often pictured with his heel lower than his toes as his foot passed through the bottom of the pedal stroke—especially on climbs.)

Studies done on Olympic cyclists show that even the best riders don't produce power on the upstroke. The pedal goes around so fast that they can't actually pull the foot up as the pedal rises. The exceptions are mountain bikers who are nearly stalled on technical terrain and amputee riders who pedal with only one leg. These riders can benefit from ankling in these cases.

CHAPTER 8

HANDS, ARMS, AND SHOULDERS

Among the three areas of contact between the body and the bike (crotch, hands, and feet), the crotch gets much of the attention. After all, a case of saddle sores is an ailment you won't soon forget.

But hand problems might be even more debilitating because we use our hands all day long for our jobs and daily activities. For a surgeon, a musician, a woodworker, or a writer, numb fingers can be career-threatening. Fortunately, tingly digits can be avoided with proper bike fit and judicious padding in gloves and handlebars.

Arm and shoulder injuries in cyclists are almost always a result of contact of another kind—with the ground. Usually, these crash-induced injuries are straightforward orthopedic cases that require only minimal healing time.

CYCLIST'S PALSY AND CARPAL TUNNEL SYNDROME

Description

Cyclist's palsy and carpal tunnel syndrome are afflictions that result in pain and numbness in fingers. Cyclist's palsy involves compression of the ulnar nerve and usually affects the ring finger and little finger. Carpal tunnel syndrome means the median nerve is affected and results in numbness of the thumb and forefinger. Job stress can play a part also, and combined with riding, the result can be a serious case of either of these maladies.

Symptoms
Riders with either of these maladies experience a tingling sensation in their hands and fingers; the hands and fingers may also become numb.

Causes
Cyclist's palsy is caused by nerves in the hand that get compressed against the handlebar or brake lever hoods. Riding with your wrist cocked and angled toward the thumb can lead to numbness in the ring finger and little finger. The flat bars on mountain bikes encourage riders to keep their wrists bent and don't allow many changes in hand position.

Riding with your hands on the brake hoods of a road bike with the wrist cocked and angled toward the little finger can lead to carpal tunnel syndrome, with numbness afflicting the thumb and index finger.

Another culprit is a saddle that is tilted down. This causes you to slide toward the handlebar, putting your weight forward and onto your hands.

Treatment
Your grip on the handlebar is the key to treating (and avoiding) cyclist's palsy and carpal tunnel syndrome. Keep your wrists straight when you grip the handlebar. Bent wrists lead to nerve entrapment and hand pain. Use a flat bar that angles to the rear so your wrist isn't bent as much. Additionally, if you're on a road bike, vary the position of your hands every few minutes from the drops to the brake hoods to the top near the stem.

Stand frequently to alter the pressure on your hands. Use gel-padded cycling gloves, cushy grips on a flat bar, or padded tape on a drop bar to relieve pressure on the nerves in your hands.

Make sure your saddle is level with the ground to keep you from sliding forward. If you feel the saddle needs to be tilted for you to ride comfortably, the reach is probably incorrect on the bike. Check Chapter 3 to learn how to get the proper reach to the handlebars.

If These Remedies Don't Work
If you're still having problems with numbness and tingling, get the weight off your hands by moving your handlebar higher and closer to the saddle. The easiest ways to do this are with a shorter stem that has more rise or (for traditional quill stems) installing a model that has a long shank.

Try additional padding on the handlebars. Specialized sells a gel-filled pad called "Bar Phat." You simply stick it to the handlebar and wrap the tape over the top.

If you use a flat bar, consider a "riser" or downhill model. This style causes you to sit up a bit more, relieving pressure on your hands.

The Importance of Cycling Gloves
Always wear gloves, even for short rides to run errands. Properly padded anatomic gloves are necessary for comfort. They protect your hands and associated nerves from road vibration and pressure from the handlebar. If you ride off-road, consider long-finger gloves for added protection.

Gloves are most valuable if you crash. The natural reaction to falling is to try to break the fall by reaching out with your hands, which means the palms of your hands have the most contact with the ground—and the worst abrasions, if you aren't wearing gloves. When palms slide across the pavement, the resulting deep cuts and abrasions are some of the most painful injuries you can imagine. They heal slowly, too, because you use your hands so much every day that it's hard to shield the cuts from being reopened.

NAVICULAR WRIST FRACTURE

Description
This wrist problem involves the fracture of a small bone on the thumb side of the wrist. It's called a snuffbox fracture. To inhale snuff, people used to place it in the indentation between two tendons that you can see at the end of your wrist when you angle your thumb up (see Figure 8.1). The pain of a navicular fracture occurs in the same place.

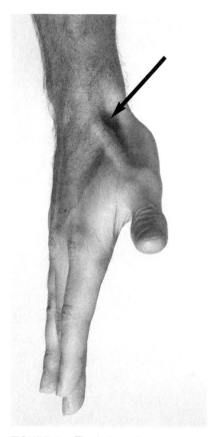

FIGURE 8.1 The indentation marks the location of a navicular fracture.

Symptom

A fracture here has one main symptom: pain on the inner base of the forearm where the wrist and thumb join.

Cause

This fracture can occur when you extend your hand to catch yourself in a fall.

Treatment

This is an especially difficult fracture to diagnose. Often there's no deformity, but it stays sore for days just above the base of the thumb and there's little or no improvement. If you have pain in your wrist, have an X-ray done, even if you think it's only a slow-healing bruise. It may take several X-rays over time to identify the fracture. It may not show up until it starts to heal.

This injury should be immobilized for several months until healing is complete. If it does not heal properly, surgery may be required. By the way, many riders have raced successfully in a navicular cast, but this should only be done at the discretion of the rider's medical caregiver.

BROKEN COLLARBONE AND SHOULDER SEPARATION

Description

A fractured clavicle (collarbone) is one of the most common cycling injuries. A shoulder separation occurs when the joint between the shoulder blade and the collarbone is wrenched apart by impact. This acromioclavicular (AC) joint (see Figure 8.2) is the bump on the top of your shoulder, about 2 inches inboard.

Symptoms

In the case of collarbone fractures, symptoms include pain and swelling of the collarbone area. You may have also heard a popping sound when you hit the ground. Often you can feel and see a bump on the collarbone that wasn't there before.

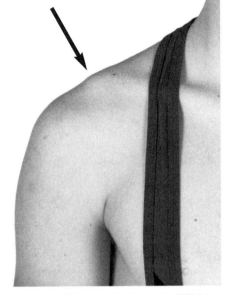

FIGURE 8.2 The acromioclavicular (AC) joint.

If you separated your AC joint, the pain and swelling may be farther out on the shoulder where the collarbone meets the shoulder blade.

A shoulder separation may result in a "step shoulder," a prominent dip of the outer inch or two when viewed from the front. Compare it to the other shoulder in a mirror to check.

Cause

Broken collarbones and shoulder separations result from a fall on your shoulder and/or on your outstretched hand.

Treatment

There is no quick fix for these injuries. Riding with either injury is dangerous because the pain and disability compromise your handling of the bike. Mountain bikers have ridden many miles of rough trails to get to medical help, and pro roadies have continued riding to finish races. But such heroics aren't recommended because they can make the injuries worse and ultimately delay healing.

See a physician immediately. Go to an emergency room or directly to an orthopedic surgeon. For most collarbone fractures, you'll have to wear a stabilizing sling or other device for a few weeks until you're comfortable. The broken ends of the bone will find each other and knit back together. (In rare cases, the ends must be pinned together.) Healing usually takes six weeks, but it's okay to ride indoors on a trainer when you can do it comfortably.

Most shoulder separations don't require surgery unless they become functional or cosmetic problems over time. The exception is a combination fractured collarbone and AC separation. When these injuries occur together, surgery is usually required.

CHAPTER 9

CROTCH AND SKIN

Until quite recently, riders sat on hard, plastic-shell saddles that weren't shaped for their anatomy. Shorts were made of wool and had a liner made of leather. This chamois was soft when new, but after a few washings, it lost its natural oil and assumed the texture of a taco chip.

We have come a long way since those days. These days, you may still find that you occasionally have problems with saddle soreness or skin rashes, but with present saddle and cycling shorts technology, you should be able to find designs that enhance your comfort and safety. It may require some trial and error, though.

SADDLES AND SHORTS

Maybe I was wrong when I said that the most personal part of cycling was the reach to the handlebar. It may actually be the choice of a saddle and shorts!

Remember that the same saddle won't work well for everyone. Just as there is significant variation in face shapes among the general population, there's a wide difference in crotch shapes as well. And there is a variety of saddle and shorts designs out there—and there will be some that are right for you. If you don't find the right combination on the first try, you just have to keep looking.

A good bike shop should be willing to switch the saddle on a bike it sold you if you can't get comfortable after a few weeks. Saddles are expensive, but you should not let this stop you from finding a model that fits your unique anatomy. To minimize the expense of trial and error, ask a shop if it has loaner saddles you can try. Or organize an informal saddle-swapping club. Find several cyclists who are willing to trade saddles or even buy new ones to pass around for others to ride. And when you finally find a saddle that works or you, buy one for each of your bikes!

Of course, for sanitary reasons, you can't exchange bike shorts after you've worn them. But if your shorts are giving you problems, don't keep wearing them. Try other styles or brands until you find the ones that work best. Once you find a liner design that works for you, buy several pairs of those shorts. If your favorite model is discontinued, look for the same general shape and stitching pattern when you need more shorts.

CROTCHITIS/SADDLE SORENESS

Description

Crotchitis and saddle soreness are general terms for soreness in the perineum (crotch), where soft tissue meets the saddle. Problems can be as simple as boils or as complicated as pudendal nerve palsy (genital numbness), impotence (erectile dysfunction), prostatitis (inflammation of the prostate gland), or urethritis (urinary tract difficulties). The symptoms and causes are all related to irritation from the contact between the seat and the crotch.

The crotch isn't designed to bear weight, but time in the saddle allows it to adapt. The soft tissue that overlays the ischial tuberosities (sit bones)—the two points of the pelvis that should contact the saddle—can take time to adjust to the added pressure.

Symptoms

Skin in the crotch can become red and irritated from friction. Sometimes it erupts in small boils or a painful rash.

Numbness can be a symptom of pudendal nerve palsy. Men can suffer from saddle-induced prostatitis or impotence, although occurrences are rare. Women may experience abraded soft tissue.

Pain and swelling directly on the sit bones are indicative of ischial bursitis (an inflammation of a bursal sac located in the gluteal region).

A feeling of bladder pressure, sometimes combined with the desire to urinate frequently, is a symptom of urethritis. With this comes irritation and inflammation of the urethra (the tube through which you discharge urine).

Causes

Crotch irritation is often caused by a poor riding position resulting from poor fit or poor saddle choice. A saddle set too high causes you to rock your hips as your legs reach the bottom of the stroke, sawing your delicate tissue across the saddle. An upward-tilted saddle causes the nose to press into your crotch, while a downward tilt causes you to slide forward and push yourself back, resulting in an irritating rub.

There is no specific saddle design that is right for every rider. The saddle that is crotch nirvana for one rider is pubic purgatory for another. Try various designs to find the one that works best for you.

Problems with your clothing can also lead to crotch irritation. It can be caused by failure to wear cycling shorts that have a well-constructed liner to pad the crotch and reduce abrasion. The biggest mistake new riders make is wearing underwear with their cycling shorts, or even not using cycling shorts at all. Additionally, remaining in your cycling shorts after a ride can lead to boils because the bacteria have time to penetrate and infect abraded skin.

Riding in rainy or humid weather often causes chafing as wet shorts rub your damp skin.

Problems can also result from poor riding habits, such as not standing enough to relieve pressure and not shifting to various locations on the saddle. Pressure from the saddle is the cause of pudendal nerve palsy. And ischial bursitis can be caused by a hard saddle, a poor-quality chamois, or riding too many miles too soon.

Treatment

First, make certain your riding position is correct. Your weight should be on your sit bones, not on the soft tissue in front of them. Be sure your handlebar isn't too low or too far from the saddle. An excessive reach makes you roll forward and sit on your soft tissue. If you're swaybacked, the problem can be worse.

If you have saddle problems on a tour when you must ride every day, slide the saddle forward 5 to 10 mm to move pressure to a new area. This change won't affect your relative position on the bike because your sit bones will automatically slide back to the wider part of the saddle.

Wearing the right shorts can also help. Always wear high-quality cycling shorts with a padded liner. Look for shorts developed with liners specially designed to reduce pressure on the nerves and blood vessels in the perineum. As soon as possible after every ride, get out of your cycling shorts and into the shower. Don't hang around and let your shorts become a petri dish. After cleaning up, put on loose-fitting garments so your skin will stay dry. Also, wash your cycling shorts after *every* use.

Try a skin lubricant to minimize abrasion. Some lubes are water-soluble, others are petroleum-based. Water-soluble lubricants are easily absorbed into the skin and easily wash off your skin and shorts. Petroleum-based lubricants have more staying power, especially in wet conditions. I recommend petroleum-based products that contain antibiotics. If you have to ride a good distance in the rain—on a tour, for example—a coating of petroleum jelly will reduce the risk of chafing.

For ischial bursitis, apply ice to the region, take NSAIDs, and rest off the bike. A cortisone injection can provide quick relief. To keep it from recurring, wear two pairs of shorts for more padding. You may want to cut a round hole in the liner of the inner pair, directly over the painful area. This helps reduce the pressure on the afflicted area by preventing it from touching the saddle with as much force.

A topical prescription medication such as erythromycin can be effective for spot treatment of sores. Bag Balm can be used to soothe chafing. This nonprescription product, developed to heal the irritated teats of cows, is available in drugstores. A large, deep, or stubborn boil may require treatment with antibiotics. See your doctor for an evaluation and prescription.

If These Remedies Don't Work

Most saddle problems can be fixed with good bike fit, so visit a competent shop, a licensed cycling coach, or a knowledgeable athletic trainer for help with fit. Remember, there's a big difference between fits for performance and for comfort. Be sure to explain your cycling goals.

Choosing a new saddle with a different shape and different amount of padding may also solve the problem.

Tight hamstrings stop you from rolling your pelvis forward to sit properly on the saddle. On the other hand, a tight low back causes you to roll too far forward, putting weight on your perineum. Consult a physical therapist for appropriate stretching exercises.

Check for a leg length inequality as described in Chapter 6.

ROAD RASH

Description

Falling off the bike and sliding along the pavement or trail often results in road rash—skin abrasions on the thigh, calf, buttocks, forearm, elbows, back, or shoulder.

Symptoms

The obvious symptom of road rash is red, oozing, raw scrapes.

Although road rash is usually superficial, breaking only the surface of the skin, there can be deeper cuts imbedded in the abrasions—depending on what you fell on. A surface called "chip-and-seal" is the worst. On this type of road, tar has been spread over existing pavement and overlaid with coarse gravel. If you fall and slide on it, the result is like a cheese grater on your skin.

Cause

You fell off!

Treatment

Abrasions must be thoroughly scrubbed clean to avoid infection and prevent "tattooing" of the skin from embedded asphalt oils. If you don't have soap, baby shampoo works well. It's often best to seek a physician or emergency room. They'll use a topical anesthetic to deaden the pain while they dig out embedded dirt and gravel. They'll also use sterile brushes, which you may not have at home, thus reducing the chance of infection.

Some cycling events offer wound-care service. If your fall happens during a race, check with medical support before you try to clean the wound yourself.

Road rash heals much faster, and with less scarring, if you keep it moist. Wash the wound gently several times a day, then apply a "wet" dressing that's permeated with antibiotic ointment. This helps the wound heal from the inside out, without letting a scab form.

To reduce pain, take acetaminophen (Tylenol) according to label directions during the first 48 hours after the injury. After this, you can switch to a NSAID if you prefer.

Be alert for signs of infection. These include redness in the wound or on its edges, fever, nausea, and perhaps swelling in nearby lymph nodes. If these signs appear, see your doctor.

If These Remedies Don't Work

Road rash is often accompanied by underlying bruises. This can lead to a systemic infection when the abrasion "communicates" with the hematoma (pool of blood) under the skin. If you experience fever or muscle aches, or see red streaks radiating from the abrasion, immediately go to your physician or an emergency room.

Untreated hematomas may turn to scar tissue or calcify, hardening so they produce pain and limit motion. Hip hematomas in particular often are undertreated and become cosmetically deforming. They need to be compressed and iced. If you develop a "saddlebag" of swelling in the hip area after a fall, see a physician. In the meantime, apply a compression wrap twenty-four hours a day for at least a week. For a compression bandage, wrap the affected area with an elastic bandage (ACE bandage). Don't wrap it too tightly—take only half the stretch out of the bandage as you wrap it around the limb.

Always get immediate medical help if you're deeply bruised and scraped. It's important to rule out injuries that are more serious and have your wounds professionally cleaned.

FREQUENTLY ASKED QUESTIONS: SKIN PROBLEMS

Q: How can I prevent road rash or lessen the consequences?
Obviously, good bike-handling skills help you stay upright in tricky situations. Practice cornering in a dirt field while wearing protective clothing. Riding a mountain or cyclocross bike off-road helps you get accustomed to how it feels to have the rear wheel slide around. Loss of traction on the road will be less frightening.

Another good drill to practice is to ride side by side with a friend on a grassy field. Go slow and practice bumping shoulders and elbows. Then when contact is made in a group on the road, you'll be accustomed to the experience. Keep pedaling when you feel contact. You'll be able to maintain momentum and ride through many bumps.

To reduce the number of abrasions you get from a fall, wear a light undershirt beneath your jersey. If you fall, the jersey will slide on the undershirt and absorb some of the friction that would otherwise abrade your skin. And wearing gloves is always a good idea because they protect your palms, a body part that is particularly slow to heal. And of course, always wear a helmet.

Also, consider shaving your legs. Racers and serious recreational cyclists shave for a number of reasons:

- Shaved legs make massage easier because the therapist's hands can rub the skin directly without irritating the hair follicles.
- Hairless legs are easier to clean after a wet and dirty ride.
- Hair creates more friction than smooth skin during a sliding fall, resulting in a worse abrasion.
- Abrasions on shaved legs are easier to scrub clean and bandage.
- Shaved legs look a lot nicer sticking out of tight Lycra cycling shorts!

For the first shave of the season, most riders use hair clippers to harvest the winter's growth. Then they shave off the stubble in the bathtub with a razor and shaving cream. Thereafter, shaving once every seven days or so should be sufficient. Consider using a moisturizing cream to prevent skin dryness.

Q: What belongs in a good crash kit to take to cycling events?

You need to have enough supplies to clean and dress all the injuries sustained in a crash from the time you hit the pavement to the time of healing. My teammate Drew Geer, M.D., an emergency room physician, recommends the following:

BASIC ROAD RASH KIT

Gauze pads	4 × 4 in.
Nonstick bandage	3 × 4 in.
Nonstick bandage	3 × 8 in.
Gauze roll	2 in.
Gauze roll	4 in.
Tape (silk or plastic to hold dressings)	1 in.
ACE bandage (dressing cover or splinting)	4 in.
Scissors for cutting dressing	
Antibiotic ointment	

Optional

Gloves (latex or latex-free) to wear when you help another rider to avoid coming into contact with someone else's blood

Chemical cold pack

ADVANCED ROAD RASH KIT

These are items typically stocked by hospitals or available by prescription. They are not readily available in drugstores. Your physician may be able to help you find them, or you may be able to find some of them on Web sites that sell medical goods.

3 mm Microdon dressing	6 × 10 cm
3 mm Microdon dressing	15 × 15 cm
3 mm Microdon dressing	9 × 25 cm
Surgilast netting	4 yd. of size #3
Surgilast netting	4 yd. of size #5 or #6
Sur-Clens soap	1 oz. vials
Lidocaine jelly (2%)	
Surgical scrub brush	

Q: *Do I need stitches?*

Every wound is different. Generally, if you have to ask whether you need them, you probably do. Dr. Drew Geer's expertise in the emergency room provides an answer to this question.

Any laceration will heal without stitches. But sutures promote rapid healing and decrease the risk of infection.

Common cycling injuries that need stitches are lacerations over the elbows, knees, and knuckles. These cuts sometimes penetrate into the joints or bursa, a lubricating sac outside the joint. When this happens, suturing is even more important. Additionally, lacerations on top of joints tend to pull apart and are therefore more likely to require stitches.

The placement of sutures depends on many factors: the location of the wound, tension on the skin, width and length of the opening, and the amount of time since the injury occurred. You can wait up to 12 to 16 hours to get stitched up, but sooner is better. After 16 hours there is too much bacteria in the wound, making it unsafe to suture. Closing bacteria inside the laceration leads to infection. The one exception to the 12- to 16-hour rule: A very large wound that wasn't closed within 16 hours could be closed after three to five days because the bacteria numbers decrease at this time.

Q: *My skin takes a beating while riding even if I don't crash. How should I prevent sunburn, slow the skin's aging process, and treat the occasional bee sting?*

You've heard it before and now you're going to hear it again: Always use sunscreen of at least SPF 30 on exposed skin.

Don't forget to use lip salve that contains sunscreen. And reapply often: Salve is easily rubbed off while drinking or from licking your lips. The lower lip is at greatest risk because it hangs fully exposed to the sun when you're riding hard and breathing with your mouth open. Worse, a drop of saliva or sweat can form on your lower lip and act like a lens to focus the sun's rays on your flesh.

Premature skin aging can be a serious issue for cyclists who spend so much time in sunlight. Avoid sunburn. Wear long-sleeved jerseys and leg warmers until temperatures rise above 65°F. If you get sunburned on a tour and have to ride the next day, wear leg and arm coverings even if it's hot. Hair-challenged cyclists might want to wear a skullcap under their helmets. Skullcaps are made of thin wicking material and don't require changing the sizing pads in the helmet.

Bees are another danger. A bee can fly into an unzipped jersey and sting you painfully before you can get it out. Zip your jersey if you notice bees in the area. Bees can fly into helmet vents, too. Wearing a bandana or head rag under your helmet can protect you from a nasty sting.

Carry with you a single-use tube (or two) of a sting-relief product, sold in drugstores. These fit easily in your jersey pocket or seat bag and can help reduce the pain if you get stung by a bee. If you are allergic to bee stings, seek medical help immediately after a sting.

CHAPTER 10

EYES AND HEAD

W HAT'S MORE IMPORTANT THAN YOUR HEAD AND EYES? PROBABLY nothing. There is nothing you want to protect more than these two parts, or your cycling days could come to a quick end. Many cyclists ride without helmets or eye protection—which is unsafe and very risky behavior. Wearing both is a simple but highly effective way to safeguard your most precious possessions.

EYE PROBLEMS

Description
The biggest risk with your eyes is that something flies in your eye—usually a bug, dirt, or a piece of gravel. It can be disruptive to your cycling, at the very least, and result in a scratched cornea or even the loss of an eye at worst.

Symptoms
The signs that you've gotten something in your eye include a burning and watering sensation in your eye. You'll have an irresistible urge to blink even though your bike handling may be compromised.

It may feel like your eyeball is scratched. And when you look in the mirror, you may see a foreign body lodged in your eye.

Causes

Foreign bodies in the eye are usually the result of not wearing cycling-specific eyewear. When it's raining, many riders take off their sunglasses because the lenses are too dark or streaked with water. But gritty water thrown up by other riders' wheels can easily get into unprotected eyes.

Additionally, at certain times of the year, or in certain places like on a road through a farm, the air contains more insects than usual. There's a greater chance of getting one in your eye.

Treatment

If you get something in your eye, stop riding. It's dangerous to continue. A foreign object in one eye often causes the other eye to squint shut in a kind of muscular sympathy.

Irrigate the affected eye immediately with water. (This is a good reason to fill at least one bottle with water rather than sports drink.) Don't delay! Blinking your eye with something in it can scratch the cornea.

To prevent eye problems, always use eyewear to deflect bugs and other airborne debris. Sunglasses also lessen eyestrain caused by squinting, and eye fatigue leads to whole-body fatigue. High-quality glasses also provide protection against ultraviolet sunlight. Remember, you can't put sunscreen on your eyeballs.

On rainy days, use clear or yellow lenses and wear a billed cycling cap under your helmet to shield your eyes from road spray.

If These Remedies Don't Work

If the feeling persists that your eye is scratched or something is still in it, see a physician.

CONCUSSION

Description

A concussion results from a blow to the head. The brain is banged against the skull, causing swelling.

Mild concussions sometimes produce a short loss of consciousness. They also can cause amnesia or emotional problems. Severe concussions result in prolonged unconsciousness and many more-dangerous symptoms. Immediate medical care is essential.

Symptoms

When you experience a blow to the head, you may be stunned momentarily but eventually feel like you can continue riding. You may also lose consciousness.

You may have seen a flash of light when your head made contact with the ground. A cracked helmet is a sign that you might have a serious head injury.

Cause

A concussion is caused by a strike to the head, such as in a crash. Sometimes your head contacts the ground first, as in a fall over the handlebars. In sliding falls on your side, your head may whiplash into the pavement.

Treatment

Stop riding, even if you feel okay after the crash. If you're alone and must ride or walk home, go slowly. You may suddenly get dizzy or find your eyes unable to focus.

Even a brief loss of consciousness means you should see a physician. If you didn't lose consciousness, see how you feel the next day. If you experience headache, dizziness, or nausea, go to your doctor or an emergency room immediately.

Do not take aspirin. If there's bleeding inside your skull, aspirin will retard clotting and can cause complications.

If you live alone, tell a friend that you hit your head and ask him or her to check on you. Generally, you should be checked on every two hours for the first twenty-four hours following the injury.

Get medical clearance before riding again.

If someone riding with you falls hard and is knocked out, stabilize his head and neck, but do it with as little movement as possible. There could be a spinal cord injury, which will be made worse by movement. Monitor his pulse and breathing until help arrives.

TIP: *Serious crashes are relatively rare in cycling, but they do happen. There's no feeling so wrenching as the one you'll get while standing helpless, not knowing what to do, while another rider lies motionless on the ground. Every cyclist should receive First Responder training as promoted by the American Red Cross. This will enable you to help yourself and others in emergencies. Update the course every two years.*

PART III

GETTING THE MOST OUT OF CYCLING

CHAPTER 11

OVERTRAINING AND RECOVERY

I'VE EXPERIENCED OVERTRAINING AS A CYCLIST. I'VE STUDIED IT as a student. And I treat athletes for it at the Boulder Center for Sports Medicine.

But I'm still not sure what overtraining is. Is it physical, psychological, or merely hype? In my experience, it's a combination of all three. Basically, overtraining (sometimes called overreaching) is a lessening of performance despite hard training. Causes include:

- Too much training (including racing) without adequate rest and recovery.
- Intense training without having gradually worked up to a sufficient number of miles.
- Poor nutrition, especially failure to consume enough carbohydrates to replenish glycogen (muscle fuel) in time for the next workout.

One thing is certain—different cyclists react to the same training program in very different ways. A genetically gifted athlete often can tolerate huge training loads and improve steadily. But when a more modestly talented rider tries to duplicate that same program, he'll probably become exhausted rather than getting faster. Additionally, what is a comfortable training load one year may be too much for that same athlete the next year, due to outside demands such as job and family.

SYMPTOMS OF OVERTRAINING

The effects of overtraining can accumulate like a snowball rolling down a hill. Typically, overtraining starts when a cyclist is feeling great, training well, and improving each week. These successes fuel his desire to train harder. He might even decide to restrict calorie intake to lose weight so that he can climb better.

Then, gradually and without significant warning signs, something goes wrong. His desire for riding decreases. He has a strong urge to quit during races. His performances get worse instead of better. Unless he knows the subtle symptoms of overtraining and takes immediate action, he'll continue to train hard—and the pattern of chronic exhaustion and poor performance will deepen.

You can see why it's vital to recognize overtraining. There are seven key signs to look for.

Steadily worsening performance. When your performance deteriorates despite hard training, it's probably getting worse because of hard training.

Depression. Psychologists have found many correlations between overtraining and symptoms of depression. In fact, William Morgan, M.D., who pioneered research on overtraining in the 1970s, once said, "I've never seen an overtrained athlete who wasn't clinically depressed." However, the exact cause-and-effect relationship is still debated in professional circles. Does overtraining cause depression, or does depression limit our capability for heavy training and high performance? The jury is still out.

Persistent soreness in muscles and joints. Cycling is a non-weight-bearing activity and doesn't involve the pounding that our bodies get in sports that involve running. For this reason, your muscles shouldn't become excessively sore even after hard rides, and they certainly shouldn't stay sore for days at a time.

Loss of appetite combined with a 5 percent loss of body weight over several days. Abrupt weight loss is usually a symptom of chronic dehydration. But it may also mean that your body lacks sufficient glycogen to fuel your training—and it has begun to devour muscle tissue for fuel.

Digestive problems including diarrhea or constipation. Chronic fatigue can cause the digestive system to function improperly.

Rise in resting heart rate. An increase of 7 to 10 beats above your normal morning resting heart rate is a classic symptom of overtraining.

Rise in white blood cell count with accompanying susceptibility to infection and illness. This can be an excellent measure of your overtraining status if you know your white cell count under normal circumstances.

> **TIP:** *Get a complete blood count so you can establish your base-line levels. Pro riders often get checked four times per year, but for recreational riders this can get quite expensive. Serious riders might consider having three blood counts per year to establish their own unique baseline levels. Even severely overtrained athletes usually don't have blood profiles that fall out of normal ranges. Therefore, it's important to establish what's normal for you so that minor variations can be spotted.*

CAUSES OF OVERTRAINING

What makes athletes drive themselves to the point of overtraining? Two popular theories suggest that being very goal oriented and being addicted to exercise may be part of the problem.

Competitive, goal-oriented people are more likely than others to suffer from overtraining. Their high levels of motivation allow them to ignore pain and discomfort. They are often individuals who like to have a lot of control, grasping for mastery in a world that seems to fly by out of their direct influence. A daily ride is something they can control, and this control is gratifying, and so they overdo it.

People can develop an addiction to physical activity, especially endurance exercise. You've probably heard the term "runner's high" used to describe the feeling runners get from exercise. This addiction has been studied for decades. During exercise, the body produces endorphins, which are morphinelike substances secreted by the brain and pituitary gland during exercise. In theory, an addiction to these endorphins drives people to train even when tired or injured.

Finally, many athletes don't consider their total stress load when they figure out how much rest they need to recover from hard training. The hours on the bike certainly count as stressors, but so does the time you spend at work, doing chores at home, and fulfilling family and social obligations.

If you have a challenging career and other demands on your time, don't make the mistake of comparing your time on the bike to that of your favorite pro rider. It's tempting to think that because the average pro cyclist spends 20 to 30 hours a week riding, a recreational rider's 6 to 10 hours of cycling couldn't possibly lead to overtraining. However, pro cyclists do little except ride and recover. They have team support staff to clean their bikes, give them massages, and do their laundry.

But time-pressed recreational cyclists have to fit time on the bike around many other demands. I bet no one is cleaning your bike for you, right? And you probably have to mow the lawn and go to the grocery store after a hard training ride. In these real-world conditions, some cyclists don't allow enough time for recovery, and overtraining results from a relatively low number of training hours.

PREVENTION OF OVERTRAINING

There are several simple techniques required to avoid overtraining. Trouble is, they seem to be very hard for many serious cyclists to implement.

Train moderately and systematically. The body doesn't like sudden increases in mileage. Plan to increase your distance gradually, and stick to your plan. There's no need to pile on massive miles, either, unless you're riding ultramarathon events. Total yearly mileage isn't related to the number of championship medals on your mantel.

Keep a training diary. If you fall victim to overtraining but haven't kept a training log, you won't have a record of what you did wrong. Record details of your daily workout, your morning body weight, morning heart rate, and a subjective rating of how you feel each day. Also include other relevant details, such as changes to your position or equipment.

Be aware of the symptoms of overtraining. Check the list given here and monitor your body (and your mind) for early indicators of trouble. When they surface, back off your training immediately!

Eat and drink enough. Many times, the cause of overtraining boils down to undereating. If you don't consume enough carbohydrates (and total calories) to fuel your training load, your muscles will fail to replenish their glycogen stores overnight. You'll build a progressively larger fuel deficit. Soon you'll be running on empty.

Also, most endurance athletes are chronically dehydrated. To avoid dehydration, drink even when you aren't thirsty. You should need to urinate every couple of hours, and your urine should be nearly clear.

Think of it this way: Training requires at least 600 calories per hour, and hard training or racing can consume 1,000 calories per hour. But how many riders eat enough to keep up with the demand? Replacing 600 to 800 calories means that you'd have to eat two whole energy bars and consume a bottle of sports drink each hour of a long ride. Most cyclists don't do that—and as a result are chronically undernourished and dehydrated.

Not only do most riders not refuel properly during a ride, they fail to eat and drink enough after hard training as well. According to the late Ed Burke, Ph.D., you need to consume about 1 gram of carbohydrate for every pound of body weight in the two hours immediately after your ride. For a 150-pound rider, that's the equivalent of two bananas, a bagel with jam, and a large glass of orange juice. Burke also recommends that for optimum recovery, each 4 grams of carbohydrate that you eat should be accompanied by 1 gram of protein. Better add a turkey sandwich to that post-ride meal!

Schedule rest into your yearly training plan. Every cyclist, no matter how enthusiastic about her sport, needs some downtime. Plan periods of a week or a month where you participate in activities other than cycling. It's fine to ride a little during this active rest, but do it only for grins and keep the intensity low.

Don't forget to have fun on the bike! A bicycle is one of the best playthings humans have ever invented. So play! If every ride is a grim-faced quest to achieve goals, you'll soon find out what overtraining is all about. And then you'll probably quit.

RECOVERY TECHNIQUES

Overtraining can be sidestepped with sound recovery techniques, too. Pro riders can go hard day after day in three-week stage races because they make a science out of recuperation.

Proper diet and hydration are important, of course. Your muscles must be well fueled for the next day's effort. But there are three other effective—and underused—recovery techniques that can make a big difference in how you feel (and ride) each day.

Leg Elevation

The simplest and most effective recovery technique takes little time and no effort. Simply elevate your legs after a ride. The lymph system, which collects liquid debris in your blood, cleanses itself more readily with the help of gravity. Just think of the lymph system as a sewer for your body. You fill it up with waste products during a hard ride, then help it drain by raising your legs.

Lie on your back on the floor or a bed, with your rear end about three feet from a wall, couch, table, or something else that's high. Raise your legs until they're at about a 45-degree angle with the floor, and place your heels against the object. Bend your knees slightly. Place a pillow under your head so you're comfortable. Relax. Ten minutes will work wonders.

Elevate your legs anytime it's possible within the bounds of decorum and decency. For instance, prop them on a chair at dinner. Watch TV in a reclining chair rather than sitting on the couch with your feet on the floor. Soon your family will get used to your unorthodox postures.

TIP: *To make use of every chance to help your legs recover from rides, follow the pro racers' rule: Never stand when you can sit; never sit when you can lie down.*

Stretching

Although some riders make a ritual of the pre-ride stretch, it isn't especially important. Stretching is more effective when the muscles are loose—which is the situation after a ride, not before. So warm up on the bike with easy spinning, do the ride, and then stretch afterward when your muscles are warm and relaxed.

Stretch slowly and gradually. The mechanism of the stretch reflex is based on a little nerve ending in the tendons called a Golgi tendon organ, or Golgi body. It looks like a coiled snake. When the Golgi body is deformed rapidly, it sends a signal to the brain for the muscle to shorten and protect itself. That's why rapid, forceful, "ballistic" stretching doesn't work.

If you deform the Golgi body rapidly, it will automatically tighten the muscle. Instead of effective stretching that produces elongation of the muscle, you'll get the opposite result when your muscles contract. On the other hand, when the muscle is warm and fatigued, the Golgi body is much more relaxed. If you go slowly, you'll get a better stretch.

For a sports-specific stretching program, consult a book on the subject. The classic in this field is Bob Anderson's book, *Stretching*. Check out www.stretching.com for more information. If you have difficulty with tendinitis or want more flexibility so you can lower your stem for better aerodynamics, you may want a stretching program that is more individualized and customized just for you. Consult a physical therapist or athletic trainer.

For stretches that target specific injuries, see Chapter 19.

Self-Massage

Massage therapy is an effective recovery tool. It works because it's a manual evacuation of the lymph system and mechanical release of muscle spasms. Any pro rider can tell you that massage is an important arrow in his quiver of recovery techniques.

Professional teams employ enough massage therapists so every rider gets a nightly session on the table. For recreational rides or tours, the massage tent is the busiest place at the finish of each day's ride. But a daily or weekly massage is expensive if you aren't a pro with a team of therapists at your disposal. Fortunately, self-massage is a good option.

Use lotion so your hands glide more smoothly on the skin. Massage oil is best, but moisturizing creams work well, too. Although shaving is a personal choice, hairless legs are easier to massage. Hair irritates your hands, and the rubbing motion can inflame hair follicles, leading to infection. Also, massage lotion coats the hair and is hard to clean off.

Sit on the floor in a relaxed position with your knees bent and your back supported. Start the massage with your toes and feet. Pay particular attention to the arch. Work on the big muscle of the calf with long, sweeping strokes from the ankle toward the knee. If you find any sore areas, take more time to knead them gently.

Spend most of your massage time on the prime movers of cycling—your quads. Again, work from the knee toward your heart with long, kneading strokes. Don't forget the hamstrings, especially in the middle of the thigh and near the top where they connect to the glutes.

CHAPTER 12

WEIGHT LOSS

PRO CYCLISTS ARE STRIKINGLY LEAN. ELITE MALE RIDERS AVERAGE as low as 3 to 10 percent body fat. Elite women average about 5 percentage points higher. Women tend to carry extra fat for genetic reasons related to energy reserves required for childbearing. Even so, hard-training women endurance athletes are now approaching male body fat percentages.

Pro riders often make a fetish out of losing weight. A low body weight improves climbing, and the improvement is greater than can be gained from many performance-enhancing drugs. A study at Marshall University showed that one pound of body weight is equivalent to a 1 percent difference in performance on a hilly course. In other words, if you lose a pound, your performance improves by 1 percent. If you gain a pound, you'll be 1 percent slower. No wonder pro riders get fanatical about their weight!

Lance Armstrong, in his book *It's Not About the Bike*, reveals that he weighs his food portions. He figures that if he can monitor the exact number of calories he is ingesting and calculate the number of calories he burns on his rides, he can create a small but significant daily caloric deficit. Thus, he can lose excess weight slowly so his performance won't suffer.

However, it can be dangerous to try to lose too much fat, or to lose it too quickly—and if your health suffers, your cycling will definitely suffer.

There are safe ways to lose weight to help you reach your ideal weight without compromising your health or athletic ability.

WEIGHT LOSS DANGERS

Several dangers can accompany attempts to reach an extremely low level of body fat.

Lack of energy to train. It's crucial to eat enough carbohydrates so your body can make sufficient glycogen to fuel its muscles. If you don't eat enough, first you'll burn excess fat. Then your body will begin to devour its own protein in the form of your muscles. And those muscles, of course, are what propel you down the road. However, you won't lose weight unless you're incurring a calorie deficit. The trick is to keep the deficit within reason. If you burn 500 more calories per day than you consume, you'll lose a pound every seven days. That's sensible.

Poor morale. Starvation is no fun. If you're suffering from hunger or are so weak from lack of food that your rides degenerate into plodding death marches, you'll lose your enthusiasm for weight loss (and for cycling) in a hurry. The result is often binge eating when your willpower evaporates. Cycling can be a hard sport. Don't make it even tougher by trying to cut too much weight too quickly.

Psychological problems such as anorexia and bulimia. In extreme cases, some cyclists may become so obsessed with weight loss that they develop eating disorders. These afflictions usually affect women, and studies estimate that about one third of college female athletes have some sort of problem eating pattern.

Psychologically predisposed men can suffer, too. About 30 percent of male athletes involved in sports that encourage a lower body weight, such as crew and wrestling, are estimated to be afflicted with eating disorders. Symptoms include episodes of binge eating, self-induced vomiting after meals, strict fasting, and a feeling of lack of control over your eating behavior. If you experience any of these, seek medical help immediately.

LOSING WEIGHT SAFELY

Is it possible to lose excess pounds responsibly and settle at your ideal cycling weight? Sure. Here's how.

Find your body fat percentage. It's possible to be overweight but not overfat. Muscular athletes, especially those with highly developed upper bodies, aren't too fat to be good climbers even though they may be quite heavy for their height. It's the extra muscle that slows them.

Because it's unwise to attempt to lose muscle tissue, it's important to know how much fat weight you can safely shed. The best way to find out is to get a body fat analysis at a university's human performance lab or at a sports medicine clinic.

Determine your ideal cycling weight. When you have your body fat measured, you'll get a written analysis telling you exactly how many pounds of fat you're carrying. Often, these programs will suggest an "ideal" weight for you. This figure is only a suggestion. You'll have to find your own best cycling weight by carefully monitoring how you feel and how well you perform at different weights. Less is definitely not better if you get so lean that you lose the muscle mass that's crucial to cycling performance.

Watch your food intake. If you're having trouble losing unwanted fat or maintaining your ideal cycling weight once you've reached it, you are probably eating too many fat calories. It's probably the ice cream. Monitor your intake and then reduce the number of calories you get from fat.

You can cut unhealthy fat significantly without major dietary changes by replacing high-fat items with healthier choices. The taste and mouth feel of the food won't be affected. Look at the list below, then make one or two of the suggested food substitutions each week. You won't notice the difference in your eating enjoyment, and cutting fat calories will help you meet your weight loss goals.

- **Whole milk.** Gradually wean yourself from whole milk by drinking 2-percent for several weeks, then graduating to skim milk. In recipes, use skim milk, or replace milk with a nonfat liquid such as fruit juice or vegetable broth.

- **Muffins and scones.** Watch out. Sure, they're tempting treats to munch with our morning java. But they can be as much as 40 percent fat. And some popular coffee shop scones contain more than 600 calories! Substitute a bagel with jam or a high-carbohydrate sports bar.

- **Butter, margarine, or oil.** Halve the amount of butter, margarine, or oil called for in a recipe and replace with an equal amount of nonfat yogurt, applesauce, or mashed banana. (Applesauce or pumpkin won't change the flavor, but banana will.) Carbonated water can be used in place of oil.

- **Sautéing.** Instead of sautéing foods with oil or butter, use sherry, wine, vegetable broth, or water. You can also sauté vegetables in a dry pan. Add a pinch of salt to bring out the water.

- **Salad dressings.** A low-calorie, healthful salad can become a high-fat nightmare when you add commercial dressing. Skip the high-fat dressing and squeeze a bit of lemon juice on the salad. Make your own dressing by adding vinegar and lemon juice to water, tomato juice, or sweet fruit juice. Some people like balsamic vinegar and maple syrup.

- **Soup's on.** Instead of eating a whole bowl of soup, partly fill your bowl with rice, then top it off so you're using chili or soup as a sauce on the rice. This approach boosts your carbohydrate intake from the rice and reduces the fat from the soup stock and the meat in some kinds of chili.

- **Snacks.** Do you reach for high-fat snacks like donuts, cookies, and nuts? Next time you have the munchies, try a low-fat, high-carbohydrate sports bar instead. When you want a high-calorie soda, opt for a sports drink.

- **Spuds.** Keep it healthy: Nix the sour cream on baked potatoes. Ladle on a little skim milk to moisten the potato, then put your vegetables on top for more taste, or use low-fat yogurt or cottage cheese instead of sour cream.

- **The pizza monster.** Scrape about half the cheese off a slice of pizza. Much of the fat in commercial pizza comes from the cheese, and most pizza makers use generous amounts. Removing half of the topping reduces the fat without compromising taste. Be careful not to scrape off the veggies too.

Raise your metabolism through training. The more you ride, the more you have to eat in order to maintain your energy and supply working muscles with glycogen. Racers in three-week tours and recreational cyclists on cross-state rides or in heavy training are often astonished at the number of calories they need just to keep going.

Boosting your mileage is a great way to elevate your metabolism. Cycling burns an average of about 40 calories per mile, meaning a century incinerates around 4,000 calories.

Incorporate mild exercise into your normal day. If you can't ride more miles due to time, use the stairs instead of the elevator. Take a brisk walk at lunchtime. Ride your bike a mile to the convenience store rather than driving the car. Skip the morning snack break and walk ten flights of stairs instead. Every little bit helps.

Commute to work by bike. Riding your bike to work is a great way to elevate your metabolism all day. The morning commute fires up your fat-burning mechanisms. The ride home in the afternoon assures that you'll be feeding more excess fat to your internal furnaces all evening and through the night.

Ride the trainer in the morning. Two or three times a week, hit the trainer or rollers for thirty minutes first thing in the morning, just before breakfast. There's no need to go hard; a moderate spin is fine. This trick is an easy way to get your metabolic fires stoked so you burn additional fat all day. After the spin, eat a sensible low-fat breakfast.

> **TIP:** *Begin weight control measures in the winter so you're closer to your ideal cycling weight when the spring training season begins. Then as you increase your training, fine-tune your weight until you find your best performance level.*

CHAPTER 13

PHYSIOLOGICAL TESTING

Every sport has performance parameters that distinguish top athletes from those who are less gifted. Basketball players pride themselves on their vertical jumps. NFL cornerbacks vie to run the fastest forty-yard dash. Linemen compete in the bench press. After many years of testing athletes, coaches and sports scientists have developed guidelines detailing what performance levels identify athletes most likely to succeed.

Cycling has a set of performance tests, too. Of course, you can enjoy riding without knowing your numbers. But if you're interested in achieving your top performance, it's important to find out how you stack up so you (or your coach) can devise a training program to help you improve.

Many cyclists use heart rate monitors when they ride. But to really get the most out of monitoring your heart rate, you need to first undergo performance testing. Knowing specific numbers will allow you to designate heart rate ranges for different levels of intensity, helping you to use energy even more efficiently. The use of power meters that measure your power output in watts while you ride can help you focus your training more exactly. For this reason, many serious cyclists choose to get tested at a sports medicine clinic or university human performance lab.

This chapter looks at some performance tests for cyclists. In Chapter 14, with the help of Neal Henderson, the Boulder Center for Sports Medicine's

Coordinator of Sports Science, we'll discuss how to convert the information you get from tests into an effective training program.

PERFORMANCE TESTING

Here's an overview of several common performance tests that are useful for cyclists.

VO_2max

The harder you exercise, the more oxygen you need to take in. But eventually you reach a point at which your body simply cannot consume or use any more oxygen, no matter how much harder you work out. This is your maximum oxygen uptake, or VO_2max.

VO_2max is a measure of how efficiently your working muscles can use oxygen, expressed in milliliters of oxygen per kilogram of body weight. Top male cyclists often have a VO_2max of 70 to 80 ml/kg. Equally fit elite women tend have a VO_2max about 5 ml/kg lower.

The ultimate ceiling on an individual's VO_2max is largely inherited, but with the appropriate workouts, you can improve your VO_2max by about 25 percent. That won't necessarily translate to a 25 percent performance improvement but will increase your cycling ability considerably. However, while VO_2max is an excellent indicator of an athlete's fitness level, it's a poor predictor of performance within a group of similar athletes. This is because even at the same VO_2max, some very economical cyclists can produce more power than others.

To improve your maximum oxygen uptake you must repeatedly work out for 3 to 5 minutes at a heart rate that is 95 percent of your VO_2max. These efforts are extremely demanding.

Lactate Threshold (LT)

Lactate is a by-product of metabolism anytime you exercise. At low intensities, the body can absorb lactate faster than the muscles produce it. However, as the intensity increases, your body reaches a point at which it can no longer remove lactate as quickly as it is produced, and lactate begins to accumulate in the blood. This is called the lactate threshold (LT).

The LT represents the highest level of exercise intensity that you can maintain for a significant period—usually 30 to 45 minutes. LT is expressed in different ways: as heart rate, power output in watts, velocity, or percent of VO_2max.

LT can be determined directly by taking blood samples at gradually increasing levels of effort and measuring the amount of lactic acid (lactate) in each. The normal amount of lactate in blood is around 1 to 2 millimoles per liter. LT is usually defined as a concentration of 4 millimoles per liter of blood. A sudden 1-millimole jump from one level of intensity to another can indicate you've reached your threshold.

Coaches or physiologists prescribe specific exercise intensity zones based on LT. You can raise your LT with a variety of interval training efforts at or slightly above your threshold pace, as well as by riding longer rides slightly below your LT.

Power at LT

Your power at LT is exactly what it sounds like—it's the amount of power you can generate at your LT over a relatively long period of time, usually an hour, as measured in watts. This is one of the best predictors of endurance performance. The more power you have at LT, the faster you will ride. Furthermore, if you have a higher power output at LT than your competition, you can go hard up a hill but stay under your LT while your opponent must go anaerobic to keep up. At the end of a race containing several hard hills, you'll have a lot more in the tank for the final sprint. Or, if your power output is high enough, you will have dropped your underpowered opponent miles before the finish line!

You can increase your power at LT by riding intervals at or slightly above the pace you ride when you hit your lactate threshold. Combine this with strength-building exercises including weight training and low-cadence, high-resistance intervals on short hills.

Economy

Speed at a given level of effort is a good indicator of economy. A cyclist who is more economical can go faster at the same intensity than a cyclist who is less economical. Economy is a combination of smooth pedaling technique, strength, and mechanical factors such as good aerodynamics and low resistance between the tires and the road.

You can improve your economy by doing pedaling drills and improving your equipment. For instance, lighter wheels, tires with less rolling resistance, a lighter bike, and more aerodynamic helmet and clothing will all increase your economy.

TESTING PROCEDURES

Performance testing is typically done similar to the procedures we use at the Boulder Center. At the Boulder Center for Sports Medicine, testing is done on a stationary bike integrated with a computer. The bike has a racing-style saddle and handlebar so riders can duplicate the position they ride in on their road bikes. Cyclists bring their own pedals, cycling shoes, and cycling shorts. Additionally, to prepare for the test, we ask cyclists to taper workouts the week before and not to eat during the three hours preceding the test.

We attach electrodes to the rider's chest so we can monitor heart rate and EKG. The electrodes are held in place with a stretchy piece of gauze shaped like a sock that is pulled over the upper body. The cyclist is fitted with a mask to breathe through that allows us to collect and analyze her oxygen use. We periodically check her blood pressure throughout the procedure.

The test starts with a low-resistance warm-up. When the cyclist is ready, we increase the resistance 20 watts every three minutes. At the end of each three-minute block, we draw a small blood sample from a fingertip (a pinprick is all it takes). We analyze each blood sample to see how much lactate has accumulated. When lactate levels start to rise abruptly, the cyclist has reached her lactate threshold (LT). At that point, we record her heart rate and wattage output.

After the cyclist reaches LT, we decrease the resistance and the rider pedals easily until she recovers. Then, to measure maximum oxygen uptake, or VO_2max, we increase the resistance more rapidly (usually every minute) until she can no longer pedal at a reasonably high rpm. The computer automatically analyzes the gases that she's breathing in and out to determine her VO_2max.

After the test, a physiologist sits down with the cyclist to go over the computer-generated charts and graphs showing her performance. We make recommendations about training zones and workout plans to help her improve.

The data you get from performance testing also can be used by your coach to set up a yearlong training program with appropriate intensity levels in each season. You need to work hard enough to get better but also avoid overtraining.

BLOOD TESTING

Blood tests can reveal if you have a deficiency that is hurting your performance. Blood tests comprise several elements, and if you're found to have numbers that are too low in certain categories, this can often be remedied by your physician with something as simple as a shot or a vitamin supplement.

Many tired or underperforming cyclists request blood tests, hoping for a simple solution that could instantly boost their performance. But such simple outcomes are rare. Most well-trained cyclists, even if their performances are in a slump, have blood test results well within the normal range.

Because a number of routine blood factors are affected by consistent training, every cyclist should get his blood tested two to three times a year to establish baseline numbers. A rider will have ranges that are normal for him, but these ranges can differ among healthy athletes, often to a large degree.

Medical professionals should interpret your numbers, so I won't include so-called normal ranges, which can be misleading. Here are the common elements of a blood test and a description of what they measure:

- **CBC** is a complete blood count. This is a collection of tests that include most of the ones listed here (see FERR, Fe, TIBC, and Sat on the next page), which monitor the blood's oxygen-carrying capacity.

- **RBC** (red blood cells) is measured in millions per milliliter of blood. Low numbers may be a sign of anemia. Training causes an increase in red cell production.
- **HG** (hemoglobin) is a protein molecule inside each red cell with an iron atom attached. The iron atom transports oxygen. Hemoglobin gives blood its red color. HG is usually measured in grams per deciliter.
- **HTC** (hematocrit) describes the percentage of blood that is solid cells. (The rest is fluid or plasma.) Dehydration can falsely increase this percentage because it decreases the amount of fluid in the blood. A high hematocrit has been linked to a performance-enhancing drug that increases the number of red blood cells. However, it is possible to have a high hematocrit even without taking this drug. Living at a high altitude and being dehydrated can also produce high readings.
- **MCV** (mean corpuscular volume) indicates the average size of red blood cells. Young, fresh cells are larger than old ones that are at the end of their usefulness.
- **MCH** (mean corpuscular hemoglobin) is the amount of hemoglobin as measured by weight in each red cell.
- **FERR** (ferritin) levels indicate the level of iron being salvaged from old red cells and put back into service. Low levels of ferritin may indicate that iron is being lost from the system.
- **Fe** (iron) is found as part of the hemoglobin inside each red cell where oxygen is transported to the working muscles and tissues.
- **TIBC** (total iron-binding capacity) measures the amount of transferrin, a protein that transports iron from your iron stores to the cells that need it. A high value indicates that the body is mobilizing iron stores throughout the body and may indicate a potential future deficit in stored iron reserves.
- **Sat** (saturation) indicates the blood iron concentration divided by the total iron-binding capacity. Values below 20 percent indicate inadequate capacity to transport iron.

The physical and mental stress of training can cause damage to the muscles, connective tissue, joints, and cell membranes. Hormone levels are also affected by these mental and physical stresses. Four tests help identify problems:

- **WBC** (white blood cells or leukocytes) is measured in thousands per milliliter of blood. White cells protect the body against disease, so their numbers usually increase with stress, infection, viruses, and inflammation. Certain vitamin deficiencies and poor diet also can affect white cell count.
- **CBC differential.** White blood cells come in several types: lymphocytes, monocytes, neutrophils, eosinophils, and basophils. The differential is the percentages of these different cells in your blood. These counts can help your physician or physiologist determine if disease is present.
- **Plat** (platelets) measures cells made in bone marrow that contain serotonin, adrenalin, and histamine. These cells adhere to damaged tissue and release their contents, causing clotting. Platelet count is measured in millions per milliliter.
- **Sed rate** (sedimentation rate) is the speed at which red blood cells settle to the bottom of a collection vessel. Damaged cells clump together so they fall faster than single, healthy cells. Elevated sed rate is usually a sign of infection.

Special tests done with your blood can measure levels of certain hormones. Because individual levels of these substances differ greatly, it's important to have your individual data collected over a year or more to establish a baseline. Common hormones that affect training include:

- **Thyroid stimulating hormone.** Low levels lead to sluggish performance.
- **Cortisol,** a steroid produced by the adrenal glands in times of stress. There are many good effects of cortisol, but an excess indicates problems with recovery.
- **Testosterone,** an androgen steroid produced by the testes and ovaries that influences growth, development, recovery, and behavior.

It is six times more prevalent in males than in females. Overtraining can suppress production of testosterone. The ratio of cortisol to testosterone is important. It's thought that elevated testosterone will improve recovery, but elevated cortisol indicates chronic stress inflammation and overtraining.

- **Estrogen and progesterone,** the female hormones. These can be affected by training, leading to a disruption of the menstrual cycle.

CHAPTER 14

DEVELOPING A PERSONAL TRAINING PROGRAM

O KAY, YOU'VE UNDERGONE THE PERFORMANCE TESTS DESCRIBED in Chapter 13. Next it's time to convert all those numbers into a training program that will help you improve on the bike. Of course you can get tested at your local sports medicine facility, discuss the results with the physiologist, then go home and formulate your own program. But if you're serious about improvement, consider hiring a personal coach.

At the Boulder Center for Sports Medicine, Neal Henderson, M.S., CSCS, is our Coordinator of Sports Science and also coordinates our personal coaching service. Neal's advice is the basis for the information provided here, and it's worth following.

THE COACH APPROACH

Many recreational cyclists and masters racers haven't seriously considered hiring a personal cycling coach. They think that coaches are only for top racers. But that's not the case. Everyone who wants to get better can benefit from a coach's input.

A cycling coach can, of course, prescribe specific workouts based on your physical talents, goals, and the time you have available to train. But more important than simply providing a training program, a good coach also presents an objective viewpoint. The coach can tell you when you're training too hard or recognize when your motivation is lacking.

That's really important because most cyclists are highly motivated athletes, and they tend to do too much, assuming that more training is better. But this often leads to overtraining and declining performances. In fact, some cyclists are not just highly motivated, they're overly motivated, emotionally attached to the sport, sometimes to a negative degree. A good coach provides a balance for this irrational exuberance.

It's important to choose a coach you are comfortable with, one whose training philosophy is compatible with your own. A good coach will talk with prospective athletes to see if they hit it off and have the same goals in the sport. For example, some riders feel compelled to do five- or six-hour slow training rides on the weekend when their competition goals involve short, fast races. If a prospective coach suggests that they'd be better served by shortening the training sessions and adding more quality work, but they can't give up the long weekend slog, this is a sign that the coach-athlete mix isn't optimum. In this case, it doesn't mean that the coach isn't a good one; it simply means that the athlete might do better with another coach.

You can also coach yourself by learning about the basic elements that go into establishing a training program.

COACHING OVER THE INTERNET

Some coaches offer "e-mail coaching" in which the athlete lives in a different location from the coach, and they set up workouts over the Internet. This has become a popular coaching strategy recently and gives athletes a wide range of coaching choices because they aren't limited to working with someone local.

Personal contact works best. There's no substitute for the coach getting to know his athlete—how he thinks, his position on the bike, his reaction to setbacks. However, e-mail coaching can be an acceptable option if the athlete gives honest responses to the coach's questions. Whether on e-mail or face-to-face, the coach-athlete relationship is a two-way street. If the athlete is open and honest about his responses to training and racing, it's much easier for the coach to pick up on problems.

The main drawback to long-distance coaching relationships is in teaching tactics, technique, and the mental ability to tolerate negative racing situations. In bicycle racing, tactics are crucial. If your coach can't see you compete or ride in a paceline with you during the century ride in which you're shooting for a personal record, he can't help you with all the subtle but important techniques that define good cycling.

DO-IT-YOURSELF
PERFORMANCE TESTING

Performance testing, as described in Chapter 13, is vital. A good series of tests tells the coach about the athlete's baseline performances and gives a pretty good idea of her potential. From these parameters the coach sets up a long-range program to build the rider's ability progressively.

Tests done in a lab setting are best. But some Internet-based coaches use do-it-yourself physiological tests because the athlete can do them unsupervised and report the results. Unfortunately, these do-it-yourself tests don't work very well. One commonly used measure is the so-called Conconi test, in which the rider, usually on an indoor trainer, progressively increases wattage every minute or two until she reaches exhaustion. A helper records the rider's heart rate and power output at each stage of the test. Then the cyclist graphs the data points, looking for a "deflection point" in the graph that is supposed to indicate lactate threshold.

But from tests in the lab, we know that only one out of four Conconi test subjects has a definite deflection point that coincides with a marked rise in lactate. As a result, this test isn't reliable for most cyclists, and the data aren't reliable for setting up training zones.

Another do-it-yourself test—involving short time trials—is done outside on the bike. A common version entails doing several three-mile time trials, riding all-out. Average heart rate is recorded and used to determine training zones. But this test is also inaccurate. The average heart rate for a three-mile effort is much higher than a lactate threshold heart rate determined in a lab, so training zones based on it are often too demanding and can result in overtraining.

Some coaches base their whole exercise prescription on the use of watt, or power, meters. Power meters allow you to quantify intensity directly and thus track your fitness accurately, which can be a great training aid if the information is used properly. But a power meter is only a tool. By itself, it won't make you faster. In fact, those extra eight ounces could slow you down!

THREE DIMENSIONS OF TRAINING

Training has three dimensions.

- **The amount of work done.** This has, in the past, been difficult to quantify. How do you compare a long, slow ride with a short, fast one? What duration equals a certain level of intensity? But with power meters, it is now easy to quantify the real demands of a given workout. For any given moment during a ride, you can simply refer to the meter to learn your wattage output. The ride's total energy demands are recorded in terms of kilojoules.

- **The physiological responses to that work.** The easiest physiological response to monitor work is heart rate, which can be easily tracked using a heart monitor. Other responses, more suitable for measuring in the lab, are VO_2max, lactate accumulation (or lactate threshold), and ventilation.

A finely honed sense of perceived exertion can also help cyclists measure their physiological responses. Experienced riders know that a ride was "moderate" or "hard" based on how they felt during the ride and the length of time it took to recover afterward. But this talent to read your body takes time to develop and is one reason that novice riders often do better with a coach.

- **The psychological responses to that work.** How did an interval, time trial, or that hard hill feel mentally? What about the workout as a whole? Are you excited to repeat it or do you dread the thought of getting back on the bike? Are you eager to compete or would you rather go for an easy spin by yourself? The answers to these and other questions are crucial in determining if a specific workout has helped you improve or has driven you over the edge into a state of psychological staleness.

Ideally, a cyclist or her coach uses all three methods of tracking her training. Then when there's a discrepancy among heart rate, wattage output, and perceived exertion, she is able to know that she was no longer getting the positive effects of training.

For instance, suppose a rider normally does five intervals up a hill that takes three minutes to climb. He knows from experience that he can average about 250 watts at a heart rate of 160. The effort feels "hard" on a scale of perceived exertion. But one day he averages only 230 watts. He can't get his heart rate over 155. Yet the effort feels "extremely hard," as though he can't get his legs to push powerfully enough to drive his heart rate higher. This discrepancy between the amount of power being produced and the physical toll that effort exacts is a clear warning that something is wrong and the workout should be terminated. Then he should rest, reevaluate his training program, and begin a new buildup at a slightly lower level of training volume and intensity.

PROGRAM PLANNING

You or your coach should take the information you get from physiological testing and use it to train for specific goals. Different events require different training because they use varying energy systems. If your goal is to ride the 750-mile Paris-Brest-Paris under 70 hours, your body has to be prepared differently than if your goal is to set a personal record in a 10-mile time trial.

Because of the vast differences among training plans for short and long events, as well as widely varying physical abilities, I won't try to provide specific training programs here. There's simply too much margin for error. You need a training program that is specifically suited to your goals and talents, not someone else's. However, there are some general guidelines that will help you set up your own training schedule.

It's important to use periodization as a training model. Periodization involves changing training volume and intensity throughout the season to avoid the problem of overload. To improve fitness, you must increase the amount and intensity of the training you do. But if you continue to increase the amount and intensity of training without rest, you will quickly reach a point of injury or exhaustion. The body has an astounding ability to adapt to stress, but that ability isn't infinite. At some point—and it varies with individuals—the body will break down, and improvement will come to a spectacular halt.

Periodization helps you avoid these problems by including blocks of increasing stress followed by recovery periods. The body improves during recovery. Your workouts are only the catalyst for improvement—actual regeneration occurs when you're resting. So rest is at least as important as the workouts you perform. As a general rule you should schedule a rest week after every three or four weeks of harder training.

Before you begin to plan your training, count back on the calendar from your goal event. Each phase of training covered here includes a suggested length of time you should stay in that phase of training. By counting back from the date of your goal event, you'll know when to begin training so that you can fit in all the necessary kinds of training and be at your peak for your most important events.

Base Training

Base training lasts 8 to 16 weeks. Assuming a season that begins in April with the most important events taking place in June or July, base training usually begins in February. Base training develops aerobic capacity and accustoms the rider's contact points (hands, feet, and butt) to hours on the bike. About 90 percent of training should be overdistance, emphasizing endurance and recovery. Include some short accelerations and short tempo or time trial-like efforts every week to maintain your speed while building your base.

Build Period

The build period lasts 2 to 8 weeks and immediately follows base training. A majority of your training miles in this period will continue to be aimed at building endurance, but 15 to 20 percent of your training time will be spent working on muscular strength and power in the form of tempo and lactate threshold intervals. Typically, tempo rides are done at about 80 percent of maximum heart rate in a gear that produces a cadence around 80 to 90 rpm. Tempo rides can be from 45 minutes to over 2 hours. Lactate threshold intervals are shorter, 10 minutes up to about 30 minutes, and done at a higher intensity of 85 to upward of 90 percent of max heart rate.

No matter how long or short your cycling event, all cycling ability is based on aerobic power. The aerobic system provides the potential for top performance in everything from criteriums to stage races. Your aerobic system is eighteen times more efficient than anaerobic metabolism (which does not use oxygen). To perform well on the bike, you have to enhance your ability to get energy aerobically. During the build period, you should work on increasing your aerobic ability.

However, you must also take into consideration what's known as the "competition effect." Adrenaline and race stress combine to make it possible for you to produce more power and have a higher heart rate in a race than in training. It's necessary to reduce your intensity in training to account for the lower heart rate and wattage output. If you race a 40K time trial averaging 300 watts and a heart rate of 170, don't train at that intensity. If you know you can climb a hill during a race at 330 watts, and you train on the same hill, cut back your wattage goal for repeated intervals by 10 to 20 percent.

You'll notice that the perceived exertion is about the same when you race at the higher intensity or train at a bit lower intensity. Failing to account for the additional motivation and heightened physiological response of competition is a major cause of overtraining.

Here are four excellent workouts to boost your all-important aerobic ability.

Tempo training. After a warm-up, ride for 30 to 60 minutes at a heart rate about 10 beats below your lactate threshold. Perceived exertion should be "moderately hard." You can also break up this workout into several repeats of 5 to 15 minutes.

Simulated time trials. One excellent workout to boost your aerobic power is two repeats of 20 minutes each done at about 5 beats below your lactate threshold or about 10 percent below your lactate threshold power. So if you normally compete in time trials at 250 watts and a heart rate of 160, do these 20-minute repeats at 230 watts and a heart rate of about 155. The lower intensity accounts for the vagaries of day-to-day training.

Long climbs. If you're lucky enough to have long, steady climbs on your training rides, you can do a climb at close to your lactate threshold intensity. Climbing seems mentally easier than doing the same intensity on a flat stretch. No long hills? You'll get the same effect riding into the wind.

Small pacelines. Riding in a paceline with two or three other cyclists, trading off at the front every 2 to 3 minutes, is a great aerobic workout. Ideally you'd go just over your lactate threshold when you're on the front and just under it while you're drafting. This "seesaw" effect is great for developing the ability to process oxygen. Paceline riding is good practice for bike-handling skills, too.

The Peaking Period

The peaking period lasts 2 to 4 weeks and directly follows the build period. You should include shorter and more intense work that simulates competition.

VO_2max intervals. Ride for short periods of 2 to 5 minutes with equal rest periods. Keep the intensity as hard as you can go for the duration. These intervals are often done on short hills.

Power intervals. Ride for short periods of 1 to 2 minutes done all-out with complete recovery between each bout.

Sprints. Do 10- to 15-second sprints with 5 minutes of easy spinning between each sprint.

These workouts place a great deal of stress on the body so be sure to include adequate rest and recovery. Your total training volume should decrease during the peaking period to accommodate the increased workload.

Tapering Phase

About 1 to 2 weeks before your important event, enter the tapering phase. Decrease your total volume of training even more, but maintain your overall intensity with tempo efforts and short interval sessions. Focus on your mental and tactical preparation for the race in the final few days.

Remember to be realistic about your training goals. Work, family, illness, and bad weather can throw a wrench into your training plan. If you can't stick to your schedule, don't stress about the missed training sessions. Simply begin where you left off and continue with your plan. Don't try to make up for missed training sessions by going extra-hard or long!

Remember: Most top athletes can perform only two days of quality training a week. Most recreational athletes make the mistake of performing too much intense training without allowing time for proper recovery. Don't fall into this trap.

RECOMMENDED TRAINING ZONES

Training zones help riders train at specific levels of intensity based on their goals for a workout. While training zones are often based on heart rate, I've chosen to describe seven different intensity zones based on perceived exertion. So in zone 1, the perceived effort is "very easy," while in zone 6, you'll want to work at an intensity that feels "extremely hard."

Zone 1—Recovery. Stay in this zone for 20 to 60 minutes. Perceived effort: very easy. Example: an easy 20-minute spin on Monday following a weekend of racing.

This zone is used for warm-ups and cool-down periods and to assist in recovery from hard efforts and racing. Recovery rides don't directly make you faster, but they are crucial in recovering from taxing efforts. If you don't recover, you won't improve.

Zone 2—Overdistance. Stay in this zone for 1 to 6 hours. Perceived effort: easy. Example: a weekly long ride, increasing total time by about 10 percent per week.

This is the optimum zone to improve base fitness and resistance to fatigue. Training in this zone improves your body's ability to use fat as a fuel source. Base training and weekly long rides should be performed at this level of effort. Ride slowly enough that you can talk and keep the pace for the whole ride.

Zone 3—Endurance. Stay in this zone for 45 minutes to 2.5 hours. Perceived effort: moderate. Example: a 2-hour ride on rolling terrain.

Training in this zone improves the ability to deliver more oxygen to the muscle cells and process more energy from aerobic sources. Specific adaptations that your body makes during training include an increase in the size and number of mitochondria (where aerobic metabolism occurs), an increased number of capillaries (which carry blood to and from the muscles), and an increased number of aerobic enzymes within the mitochondria.

Zone 4—Tempo. Stay in this zone for 15 to 50 minutes of continuous effort or for long intervals of 10 to 15 minutes that total 40 to 60 minutes of effort. Perceived effort: somewhat hard. Example: a 10-mile tempo ride or a long climb.

Training at this intensity will improve your ability to maintain a high pace for a long time. Power output should be slightly lower than you'd maintain in a competitive 40K time trial.

Zone 5—Lactate threshold. Stay in this zone for intervals of 5 to 15 minutes for a total of 20 to 45 minutes. Perceived effort: very hard. Example: 3 repeats of 5 minutes at your lactate threshold with 3-minute recoveries.

Training at this intensity will raise LT as a percent of VO_2max, increase your speed at LT, improve your race pace and economy, and improve your ability to withstand high levels of lactate. For time trials, your power output at LT is closely related to race performance; improve your power output and you'll improve your ability to ride against the clock.

For climbing, your power output at LT divided by your body weight produces your power-to-weight ratio, which is a good measure of climbing ability.

Zone 6—VO$_2$max. In this zone do 2- to 5-minute intervals with equal amounts of recovery for a total of 10 to 20 minutes. Perceived effort: extremely hard. Example: 5 repeats of 2-minute intervals done as hard as possible with 2-minute recoveries.

This is the optimum zone for improving VO$_2$max. This training leads to an increase in stroke volume (the amount of blood the heart pumps with each beat) and improved lactate tolerance.

Zone 7—Speed and power. Do short intervals of 10 to 60 seconds with complete recovery. Perceived effort: extremely hard. Example: repeats done on hills or sprint intervals.

Training in this zone increases anaerobic capacity and ability to handle high levels of lactate.

> **CAUTION!** *It's easy to overdo workouts in zones 6 and 7. Never do them without first building an adequate base with 8 to 12 weeks of aerobic riding. Be sure to rest appropriately. Your recovery time will be longer with these intense workouts, so monitor your body for signs of overtraining (see Chapter 11).*

CHAPTER 15

HEALTH MAINTENANCE

Staying healthy is, of course, an important part of cycling. With a good diet, vitamin supplements, and careful attention to the signs that you should stop and give your body a chance to recover from illness, you'll get much greater enjoyment out of cycling. (And probably do better in races, too.)

VITAMIN SUPPLEMENTS

Under normal circumstances, cyclists get all the vitamins they need from their daily meals. After all, bike riders eat enormous amounts! You may be loath to spend your hard-earned cash on pricey vitamins.

However, think of vitamins as "insurance." By taking a supplement, you're ensuring that your body gets the vitamins that are crucial to good health. Look for a daily vitamin supplement that contains antioxidants (vitamins A, C, E, and beta-carotene), which can help recovery. Additionally, both men and women should take a vitamin that contains iron.

Men have been warned to avoid iron supplements because of the danger of storing excess iron (hemochromatosis), but the risk has been overstated. Less than 1 percent of the population has this condition. If you have a family history of the disease or other concerns, consult your physician.

Women should also take calcium. Premenopausal and menstruating women require 1,000 to 1,500 milligrams of calcium per day. A good diet should be enough, but some women like to supplement with two TUMS® per day after their evening meal. This provides a safe insurance of adequate calcium. After menopause, check with your physician about the need for hormone replacement therapy and calcium supplements. For more information about antiaging hormone supplements, see Chapter 16.

RIDING THROUGH ILLNESS

Even with the best nutrition and a daily dose of vitamin supplements, every cyclist gets sick sometime. In fact, trained endurance athletes are more likely than their sedentary counterparts to become ill, usually with upper respiratory tract infections (URTI). Studies of marathon runners show that the risk of infection rises dramatically during the forty-eight hours after the hard and protracted effort of running twenty-six miles. Their bodies' reserves are used to recover, leaving little energy to fight infection.

No one wants to lose training time (or the fun of riding) because of nagging illnesses. When is it safe to ride through an ailment? And when is it best to take a break from riding in the interest of your health? If you catch a cold (also called an upper respiratory tract infection), here's how to recover quickly.

Rest. You have plenty of responsibilities, probably a job and family, and you don't have time to rest. A day or two in bed? Forget it. But colds respond to rest because some quality loafing gives the body extra energy to fight infection. Cut back on your work hours, take a sick day, ask your spouse to take over the dishwashing chores—anything to get a little more downtime when you're trying to recover.

Drink lots of fluids. This is good advice at any time (most cyclists are chronically dehydrated), but it's especially important when you have a cold. Water is good, but drink fruit juices too, especially orange juice for added vitamin C.

Return to training gradually. If you miss one week of training, restrict yourself to easy spinning for one week. Then gradually return to the mileage and intensity you were doing before you got sick.

> **CAUTION!** *Nearly all over-the-counter cold remedies contain pseudoephedrine, a stimulant that is also a banned substance in cycling races. Usually, taking a cold remedy will mean that you'll test positive for drug use in a drug test. Drug testing isn't limited to elite athletes. Anyone competing at a USA Cycling–sanctioned event can be tested at any time.*

For riders not concerned about medical controls at major races, it's okay to take a cold remedy to feel better for the activities of daily life. Taking a cold medicine is also appropriate when you're on a tour and need to quell cold symptoms to get through each day. Ride slow and easy so your body has the energy reserves to recover from the illness.

Because cycling is enjoyable, riders usually find it hard to take time off the bike when they're ill. When is it safe to ride—and when are you better off staying off the bike to rest and down the fluids?

Follow the above-the-neck rule. When cold symptoms are above your neck (like a stuffy, drippy nose), it's okay to exercise lightly. But when symptoms are below the neck (such as muscle aches, chest congestion, cough), don't ride. If you feel sick and puny, it's often better to rest and recover. In the long run, you'll be farther ahead by taking off several days or a week to get better before you resume training. Training through a bad cold or the flu will slow your recovery, and it will take longer to return to your best form.

CHAPTER 16

AGING AND
THE CYCLIST

THE AVERAGE AGE OF CYCLISTS IS STEADILY INCREASING. THIS "graying of the peloton" is evident in local group rides, in the average age of riders who attend cycling camps, and in the demand for more comfort (along with performance) in bike frames, saddles, and components. But even though we aren't youngsters anymore, we still want to ride like we're 25.

The body doesn't work that way, however. As we pass 30, we begin to lose some important physical attributes like ability to process oxygen, muscular strength, and sprint speed. But—and this is an important point—if you continue a program of vigorous exercise, you can slow these performance losses markedly. You can't achieve eternal life by riding a bike, but you can postpone the inevitable physical deterioration to a remarkable degree.

For example, studies have shown that in people who are sedentary, VO_2max (or maximum oxygen uptake) declines at a steady 10 percent per decade after age 40. Moderate activity can slow that decline measurably. And intense training, including vigorous cycling, can slow the loss of VO_2max to less than 5 percent per decade. A few study subjects were able to maintain, and even increase, their VO_2max into their seventh decade of life.

Muscular strength is another victim of aging. It seems to decline fairly steadily until about ages 55 to 60 then plummet much more rapidly. But continuing a lifelong and consistent program of resistance exercise can slow the loss of strength.

You don't need a gym membership or a basement full of weight machines to retain your youthful strength. Even body weight exercises like push-ups, pull-ups, and crunches are helpful. Using light weights so you can do at least fifteen repetitions of an exercise is a good way to reduce the risk of injury. As with any weight training program, consult a certified personal trainer or coach certified by the National Strength and Conditioning Association for a personal resistance training plan.

Another fact of aging is the inevitable accumulation of body fat. Multiple prospective studies of master athletes (50 to 82 years of age) showed a significant 2 to 3 percent increase in body fat regardless of whether the athletes remained competitive.

Here in Boulder, I see many extremely fit cyclists who are in their fifties, sixties, and even older. Many were racers in their youth, some on national or professional teams, and they don't want to slow down. Some of them haven't slowed down much at all!

But even though intense exercise can prolong our ability to perform at high levels, many riders want to know if there are any supplements, vitamins, or hormones that can help push back the curtain of aging—and increase their ability to recover from daily training. To find out, I consulted Michael Zeligs, M.D., an international expert on aging. He has worked as a consultant with a number of supplement companies and is the founder of BioResponse, L.L.C., of Boulder, Colorado. His advice is the basis for the information in this chapter.

In general, it's a personal decision whether or not to take supplements. Good nutrition, sound health practices, and a sensible training program do an excellent job of delaying the effects of aging, so some riders prefer getting their total nutritional package from food. However, Dr. Zeligs's ideas represent cutting-edge work in this field, so they're worth our consideration as we plan how to ride into our old age.

Please note that the views, opinions, and advice in this chapter are primarily those of Michael Zeligs, M.D. Although Dr. Zeligs is a practicing physician, I strongly recommend that you consult with your own physician before embarking on an antiaging supplemental program.

"Good recovery from intense exercise begins with simple nutritional practices," Zeligs says. "The most important is to take in sufficient carbohydrate and protein in a ratio of about 4 grams of carb for every 1 gram of protein. A number of recovery drinks on the market have this ratio, as do sports drinks designed for use while riding. So to improve recovery, use the sports drinks before, during, and after exercise."

SUPPLEMENTS

Zeligs also suggests taking omega-3 fatty acids, carnitine (or acetyl-L-carnitine), and absorbable diindolylmethane (DIM). These supplements help to support metabolism and to resolve chronic inflammation.

Omega-3 Fatty Acids

Omega-3 fatty acids are found in fish, especially salmon, sardines, and swordfish. The polyunsaturated fat found in fish oil helps prevent heart disease, so the American Heart Association recommends eating at least two servings of fish per week. Taking daily supplements of omega-3 oils with meals boosts your intake.

As an aerobic athlete, a cyclist depends on fat metabolism as a primary energy source. Stored lipids or "fatty acids" represent over 90 percent of aerobic fuel reserves in fit individuals. Long-distance cycling depends primarily on the release and metabolism of fatty acids. Because elevated levels of insulin cause the body to stop metabolizing fats, you need to remain sensitive to insulin so you can release and use stored fat while preserving glycogen or carbohydrate stores. Omega-3 fatty acids help maintain that ability to use stored fat upon which endurance athletes depend.

The opposite of this is seen in adult-onset diabetes patients who are resistant to insulin. These people have been shown to have low tissue and membrane levels of omega-3 fatty acids. Healthier people without insulin resistance have higher levels of the omega-3 fats in their tissues, especially muscles. Maintaining a high intake of omega-3s helps your body function with lower average insulin levels and greater insulin sensitivity.

During exercise, this allows preferential burning of stored fat and preservation of carbohydrate stores needed during high-effort bursts. Also, basic omega-3 fatty acid supplements help support mood. Problems with mood and energy levels after hard training are real, and omega-3 fatty acids help to lift your mood and help you maintain a good mood. Finally, the omega-3s are now understood to have an anti-inflammatory effect on muscles, ligaments, and joints.

Supplemental omega-3 fatty acids can be taken in the form of pure fish oil capsules. A typical dose is one 1,000 mg capsule, taken three times daily with meals. This can be increased to two capsules three times daily during intense training. In conjunction with a healthy diet, supplementing with omega-3 fatty acids seems safe. However, check with your physician first: Omega-3s have anticlotting qualities and so you should never take them if you're on anticoagulant medication.

Carnitine and Acetyl-L-Carnitine

Carnitine is a water-soluble nutrient that helps improve fat metabolism and maintain our body's production of energy during exercise. Carnitine helps carry the basic units of stored energy from fat into mitochondria. In this way, carnitine supports mitochondrial function. The mitochondria are specialized structures within every cell that produce molecules of ATP (adenosine triphosphate). ATP transfers energy to our muscles and is the energy currency for aerobic metabolism. Supporting tissue levels of carnitine using supplements can help to maintain efficient metabolism during exercise. Carnitine is also available as a more soluble derivative called acetyl-L-carnitine. Like carnitine, acetyl-L-carnitine supports mitochondrial function, but passes more easily into various tissues, including brain tissue. Along with omega-3 oils, acetyl-L-carnitine is a natural anti-inflammatory. Carnitine and acetyl-L-carnitine can be taken together as dietary supplements.

The recommended dose for carnitine or acetyl-L-carnitine is 500 mg per day. This can be increased to 500 mg taken three times daily during training. Carnitine supplements can be taken with omega-3 supplements. Importantly, carnitine should not be taken in the evening as it may interfere with sleep.

Diindolylmethane

Diindolylmethane (DIM) is a natural substance found in cruciferous vegetables, like broccoli, cabbage, and brussels sprouts that also improves metabolism. Taken in an absorbable formulation, DIM is active in adjusting the balance of estrogen metabolites, which then influence the behavior of testosterone. Estrogen and testosterone are hormones that are active in both men and women. With aging, activity and levels of these hormones change.

DIM has proven to be a powerful natural substance to support and maintain healthy estrogen metabolism. In women and men, DIM promotes more active conversion of estrogen to 2-hydroxy estrogen metabolites. These 2-hydroxy estrogens are known as the "good estrogen" metabolites because they support fat metabolism. They also provide protective antioxidants, which are known to prevent various forms of cancer. In women and men, DIM helps to convert active estrogen into the "good" metabolites. Since 2-hydroxy estrogen metabolites are the most tightly bound hormones to carrier proteins, these metabolites then free up testosterone by bumping it off the protein carriers. The end result is a healthier balance of "free" or unbound testosterone and less "unmetabolized" or unfavorable estrogen. Free testosterone is more biologically active to support the brain and muscles. In scientific studies, higher levels of free testosterone and low levels of estrogen have been linked to lean body mass, efficient fat-burning metabolism, and low abdominal obesity. Stimulating estrogen metabolism with DIM is effective at maintaining a balance of estrogen metabolites that favors 2-hydroxy estrogen metabolites.

New research has discovered an anti-inflammatory aspect of DIM's activity. This action may help endurance athletes to selectively metabolize fat and conserve carbohydrate (glycogen) reserves.

Absorbable DIM supplements are typically taken once or twice a day. Each dose should be between 75 and 150 mg of absorbable DIM (BioResponse-DIM). BioResponse-DIM is the only formulation shown to have adequate absorption in clinical studies. Athletic training is benefited by DIM supplements taken twice daily, with breakfast and one hour before workouts. DIM supplements can be taken along with omega-3 capsules and carnitine. As with other supplements, absorbable DIM is best taken with food.

HORMONAL BALANCE WITH AGING

As we age, maintaining hormonal balance is important to staying healthy. For both men and women, healthy estrogen metabolism is central to this balance. During perimenopause, the years right before menopause, or about ages 35 to 50, the chief hormonal imbalance that women face is estrogen's dominance over testosterone. In women, estrogen production actually rises during these years.

This is also the case with men after 50 years of age. Men go from being testosterone-dominant in their twenties to, in many cases, experiencing rising estrogen production in their fifties. This is a result of the conversion of testosterone into estrogen. With aging there is an accumulation of abdominal fat, which is the source of unwanted aromatase enzyme activity. This enzyme causes the conversion of testosterone to estrogen. Aromatase enzyme activity also increases as a consequence of chronic inflammation. So, as men in middle age tend to lose their optimal body composition, they convert more of their testosterone into estrogen. From a hormonal balance standpoint, this makes older men resemble perimenopausal women who are estrogen-dominant due to overproduction of estrogen. The difference between men and women in this regard is that men remain estrogen-dominant, similar to perimenopausal women, as they get older, but women eventually go through menopause and become estrogen-deficient.

The common thread that connects aging intervention medicine and performance in the older athlete is the role of estrogen. Higher production of estrogen and unfavorable estrogen metabolism are a problem because they prevent you from maintaining your optimal body composition. Researchers are focused on developing ways to maintain hormonal balance through more active estrogen metabolism. Increasing estrogen metabolism in the pathway of 2-hydroxy estrogen metabolites actually helps your body release and metabolize stored fat. DIM supplement can help promote and maintain this favorable estrogen metabolism.

Due to conversion of testosterone into estrogen, the use of testosterone supplements by middle-aged men is not recommended. Using these supplements can produce a dramatic increase in estrogen. The exception is older male athletes in their seventies who have become hypogonadic and ceased to produce their own testosterone. They may need to take testosterone replacement, but this is something that should be discussed with a physician first.

DHEA (Dehydroepiandrosterone)

As men and women age, there's also a dramatic loss in production of another hormone, dehydroepiandrosterone (DHEA), produced in the adrenal glands. In younger athletes, DHEA is normally produced each time the stress hormone cortisol is released from the adrenal glands. Studies done on younger athletes show that when they were involved in stressful athletic activities, their DHEA levels increased dramatically. This is a basic response to exercise in young athletes. In a younger athlete, high levels of training can lead to increased stress and the accompanying release of cortisol; it's simultaneously balanced by a secretion of DHEA.

With aging, there's inevitably a loss of the part of the adrenal gland that is the source of DHEA. One zone of the adrenal gland ages more quickly than the rest of the body, causing you to lose the cells that produce DHEA.

This means that if an older male athlete overtrains, cortisol levels go up but DHEA levels can't go up. He ends up with an imbalance in the cortisol/DHEA ratio. Elevations in cortisol not balanced by elevations in DHEA can lead to muscle loss and depressed immunity. This is a powerful argument to supplement with DHEA in the older athlete.

The concern with supplementing with DHEA is that your body can convert some of it to estrogen, which you don't want more of. But if men use DHEA in combination with an absorbable DIM supplement, then they can experience the benefits of DHEA in the presence of a healthy estrogen balance.

For women, the basic connection between DHEA and DIM is the same. DHEA supplements taken in combination with an absorbable DIM supplement help with the metabolism of estrogen produced from the DHEA. It also offers women a safer approach to the use of supplemental estrogen, should they choose to do so, when they're past menopause.

The message here is simple. Estrogen metabolism can be modified. It's not something you're stuck with because of genetics or aging. Both men and women can adjust their metabolisms in beneficial and safer directions through diet, aerobic exercise, and supplementation with DIM and DHEA.

Here's an important point: Many athletes don't want to take a supplement that they think might enhance their actual performance during a competition. They are opposed ethically to gaining an advantage over other athletes by what they view as artificial means. However, neither DIM nor DHEA should be viewed as a performance-enhancing substance. They do not affect performance or muscle mass. Instead, they promote hormonal balance, support successful training, enhance recovery, and fight the effects of aging.

Typically, women take 10 to 20 mg of DHEA per day and men take 20 to 50 mg per day in conjunction with absorbable DIM. Women should be alert to unwanted testosterone-like effects from DHEA such as increased facial hair. Men should be cautious of DHEA's possible contribution to aging-associated prostate gland growth. When taking DHEA, men should follow the status of their prostate health with the help of a physician and periodic testing for Prostate-Specific Antigen (PSA).

CHAPTER 17

COMFORT AND PERFORMANCE—YOU CAN HAVE BOTH

MOST PEOPLE WHO DON'T CYCLE THINK THAT RIDING A BIKE must be supremely uncomfortable. "How can you stand to be bent over like that?" they wonder. "And what about that skinny little seat?" Unfortunately, some cyclists also equate pain with riding a bike. This simply should not be the case.

The promise of greater comfort was one reason that the invention of mountain bikes started a second bike boom in the early 1980s. In spite of their name, most mountain bikes were ridden on the road or on bike paths. They were an innovation because they let casual cyclists sit more upright on a comfortable saddle and dampened the vibrations with their fat tires.

Road cyclists and road bike designers have been slow to realize that comfort and performance can go hand in hand. A major reason is that their idols—professional riders—are on bikes that encourage a long, stretched-out position with handlebars set much lower than the saddle. If the pros can get low and aero, so the thinking goes, recreational riders should adopt that position as well. The result has been injury and a level of discomfort, especially on long rides, that quickly drives less-committed riders out of the sport.

But now we're experiencing what Mike Sinyard, founder and president of Specialized, calls a paradigm shift. Bike manufacturers have realized that improved ergonomics leads to high performance on the bike. There is no reason to compromise comfort for the sake of performance.

To support his view, Sinyard points to pro-level Specialized frames like the Roubaix that employ compact geometry and carbon tubes with embedded elastomer inserts to dampen vibrations. This bike has been used successfully in European races like the Paris-Roubaix on incredibly rough cobblestone roads. The same bike is available to any rider who wants to tame the potholed local pavement.

Ben Serotta, founder of Serotta Bicycles and the Serotta Size Cycle, agrees. Some of his frames, like the Ottrott, use carbon tubes because they dampen vibration better than metal tubes and increase the comfort level without sacrificing stiffness. "At the end of a long ride on rough roads a carbon bike will feel better than steel or aluminum."

"I was at [former Motorola Cycling Team physician] Max Testa's human performance lab and saw a force plate they used to create vibrations," says Serotta. "You stand on it when it's vibrating and that uses lots of energy. It was invented by a guy who realized that standing during an earthquake made his legs tired! The same is true when you're on a stiff bike that doesn't absorb shock well. The mini-eccentric contractions are fatiguing and rob you of your power."

CHANGING BIKE DESIGN

Of course, as we've seen in the bike fit section of this book, comfort and performance are most easily combined if bike fit is optimal. But some bikes are designed in such a way that it's virtually impossible to get a comfortable fit.

A good example is a bike with a frame that is small for the rider's height, a low front end, a lengthy top tube, and the steerer tube cut off with no spacers between the stem and the headset. A bike like this might have the handlebars set 8 to 12 cm or more lower than the top of the saddle, and most riders don't have the flexibility to get comfortable or the core strength to stabilize their body in this position. This is especially true if the low handlebars are also set far from the saddle. Yet this design is common in "pro" bikes.

According to Serotta, "Most bike designers are young, flexible, and strong and they think that's the way bikes should look. Or the designers are people who think they're young."

Lennard Zinn, who builds frames for tall riders over 6'3" and is the technical editor of *VeloNews* and author of *Zinn and the Art of Road Bike Maintenance* and *Zinn and the Art of Mountain Bike Maintenance,* agrees. "Comfort and performance are very compatible. You can't have performance for long without comfort. Short distances are no problem—you can tolerate almost anything for half an hour—but comfort increases what physiologists call 'economy' while riding. Comfort increases aerodynamics too because if you're comfortable on the bike, you won't shift around and catch a lot of wind."

New developments in bike design and components have made the problem of poor saddle-to-handlebar differential even more prominent. "With the advent of threadless headsets," says Serotta, "handlebars lost 3 to 4 centimeters of adjustment and height compared to conventional headsets, threaded steerer tubes, and quill stems. Integrated headsets lowered them another centimeter. All this has lowered front ends even more than ten years ago (with conventional components), and they were too low then!"

This is a problem for today's aging peloton because people get less flexible as they get older. In general, older riders are pretty tight, and they're only getting tighter.

The first revelation Serotta had during his thirty years as a bike designer was that "comfort improves efficiency and, to some degree, power output as well." This led him to develop the Serotta Size Cycle and Fitting System that's now used extensively in bike shops around the world.

A Serotta fit begins with the bike fitter questioning riders about their goals and the type of riding they do. Then riders are administered a test of core strength and flexibility. The two attributes go together to establish a range of motion and control for the rider's upper body. "If a rider sits on the bike with his hands on the hoods and we could somehow remove the handlebars suddenly, some riders would stay right where they are but other riders would fall forward due to poor core strength and low back weakness."

Another way Serotta says poor core strength can be identified is by looking at a racer's position on the bike at the end of a long ride. "At the start of the race or long training ride they have a neutral spine with the vertebra in the center of their range of motion and a good position, but as the muscles fatigue they slouch on the bike, developing a rounded back and moving their hands up to the tops of the bars."

One way to make frames fit better is to use an extended head tube. Zinn says, "I did my first head tube extension on a bike in 1991. I saw a picture of a Colnago built for a tall Dutch rider named Edwig von Hooydonck. I thought it was a good idea, and now it's widely copied."

Another way to raise the bars for a more comfortable fit is to use a sloping top tube. Zinn, Serotta, and Specialized, among many other frame builders, do so, and while it's not a traditional design, Serotta says that "sloping top tubes, if done correctly, can help compensate for the low stack height of a threadless headset and stem combination, and now it's an accepted look."

Serotta uses the extended head tube as well and often uses it in combination with the sloping top tube. "By utilizing the potential attributes of a sloping top tube, we can design a bike with enough stand-over height and proper handlebar placement," says Serotta.

PROPORTIONALITY

Another comfort and performance issue is what Zinn calls "proportionality." Frames, cranks, and the width of the stance should be proportional to the size of the rider. Frames have always been available in different sizes, but most conventional cranks come in lengths ranging only from 165 mm to 180 mm. Zinn has experimented with much longer cranks— up to 220 mm—but has had to redesign the bike in order to do so.

Stance width is only slightly adjustable with the components available today. Cleats can be moved slightly in or out on the shoe, a few spacers can be used between the pedal and the crank, or a 1 cm pedal axle spacer can be used. But a petite 5'0" rider with narrow hips needs a different stance width than a 6'5", 280-pound rider with wide hips. The stance width on modern cranksets is getting wider, with no accommodations for today's smaller riders.

So it's obvious that to perform at your best, you need to be comfortable on the bike. That means a good bike fit—but it also means a frame design that allows you to position both the saddle and the handlebars in a position that is biomechanically efficient. Depending on your flexibility and core strength, that may mean having the bars only an inch or two below the saddle—or even at the same height or above. The additional comfort and improved performance you get from this will more than compensate for what many riders may perceive as less style.

SADDLE DESIGN

Long-distance performance also means finding a comfortable saddle. Nothing limits the distance you can ride like severe crotch discomfort and saddle sores. And for men, numbness "down there" can be a miserable—not to mention terrifying—experience.

For most of the history of cycling, some pain was simply accepted as part of the price you paid for riding. Saddles hadn't changed much in the hundred years the sport had been in existence. But in the past seven years, saddle design has changed dramatically. To find out the latest in crotch comfort, I discussed saddle design with Roger Minkow, M.D., a pioneer in this area and designer of the Specialized Body Geometry line of saddles.

Minkow became interested in anatomic saddles in 1997 when erectile dysfunction in cyclists hit the headlines. The publicity was due to the work of Irwin Goldstein, M.D., a urologist who examined penile blood flow in cyclists and discovered that sitting on a bike seat could reduce circulation and might lead to impotence.

However, Minkow recognized that the method Goldstein used to determine blood flow couldn't be done while the subject was actually pedaling a bike, only while he was sitting stationary on the saddle. So cycling got some bad publicity for several years, but the studies were flawed. Despite the flaws, Minkow correctly saw the need for a saddle designed to relieve pressure on the crotch, even before adequate studies could be performed. His early Specialized Body Geometry saddles quickly became best-sellers.

However, with a road riding boom under way, it was only a matter of time before better data became available.

"Now we have a way to measure penile blood flow while actually riding," Minkow says. "It was developed by Frank Sommer, a German professor who has tested hundreds of riders with many saddle designs and in riding positions ranging from sitting straight up to an extreme aero position." This research has proven to be crucial, and Minkow went to Germany to work with Sommer. What they discovered led to new and better designs.

"With the conventional saddles of ten years ago, blood flow while riding would be only 20 to 40 percent of what it was while not on the bike. But with the new saddle designs, we can increase that to an average of 80 percent for all riders using Body Geometry saddles."

So it should be a simple matter to figure out what saddle works best for a rider, right? Simply check the test results and pick the saddle that rates the highest in keeping blood flowing. But unfortunately, it is not always so easy. Minkow points out that the actual amount of blood flow varies with the rider. "Casual recreational riders are more at risk than racers," he argues. "Racers are usually quite light so they support less weight on their soft tissue when they sit on the saddle. They have great riding technique, too, which means that they stand frequently and take the weight off their perineal area.

"Finally, they're frequently racing or training at high intensity. Because they're pushing down so hard, that tends to lift their hips off the saddle slightly on each pedal stroke. In contrast, a casual rider may be overweight, he probably sits down almost the whole ride, and he's just spinning along with his full weight on his soft tissue. That can lead to an increased incidence of numbness and crotch discomfort."

So how can a rider know if he's compromising blood flow and is in danger of impotence? Of course, discomfort is one sign, but it's not the whole story.

Minkow says, "We'd like to be able to tell riders that if they get numb, that's a sign that their saddle isn't right for them. But it isn't that simple. There's no one solution to a complicated problem."

However, Minkow offers some useful guidelines for men who want to avoid problems while still riding as much as they like. First, soft, thickly padded saddles don't work. The ischial tuberosities (sit bones) tend to push the soft gel or padding down, and it wells up between the sit bones, creating more compression right where you don't want it. Additionally, saddles with grooves and cutouts can be effective, but only if they are designed properly. A poorly thought-out saddle with a hole in the middle can be responsible for a reduction to only 10 percent of normal blood flow!

Second, saddles should be the correct width for your sit bones. Generally, larger riders have wider sit bones and need a wider saddle, but this isn't always the case. Here's an area where saddle designers have let riders down. We know that feet come in different widths and so we demand that shoe manufacturers provide shoes to match. But saddles have historically always come as "one size fits all." Specialized Body Geometry saddles are now available in three widths to accommodate riders with different pelvis structures. Minkow expects other manufacturers to follow suit.

Proper bike fit is crucial. The saddle should be the correct height. If it's too high, your hips will rock on each pedal stroke, sawing the perineal area over the saddle's nose and creating unwanted pressure. Also, the top of the saddle should be horizontal to the ground. In rare cases a rider might want to tilt the nose down a degree or so (see Chapter 2 for more information). Saddles with the nose tilted up are certain to press dangerously on soft tissue.

If you feel discomfort or numbness during a ride, stop riding! Get off the bike and adjust the saddle or focus more on technique—stand frequently, for instance. When seated, move to the wider and more supportive rear of the saddle when you're climbing. One pro rider says that if he feels discomfort, he merely rearranges his parts so they sit on the other side of the nose of the saddle. This may not work for you, but it's worth a try.

And last, don't worry about the weight of a particular saddle. A comfortable model with moderate padding and a well-designed shell and cutouts may weight 40 grams more than a narrow and unpadded superlight saddle. But 40 grams is a negligible weight to carry up a hill. Training makes you faster, not saving a few grams of weight on equipment. And you can't train well if your exotic saddle is so uncomfortable that you can't log a substantial number of miles.

CHAPTER 18

THE BIOMECHANICS
OF CYCLING

THE FIT GUIDELINES IN THIS BOOK WOULDN'T BE POSSIBLE without a solid knowledge of cycling biomechanics. Biomechanists have made great progress in determining exactly what goes on in the human body when a cyclist converts energy into forward motion through the medium of a two-wheeled machine. As a result, I've already touched briefly on some of the material in this chapter elsewhere in the book, for instance, the question of foot alignment on the pedal. But this chapter expands on the biomechanics of cycling and puts all the information together under one roof.

First, a little history. Years ago bike fit was established based on static formulas found in the Italian Cycling Federation manual known by its acronym, CONI. These fit formulas had been handed down through six or seven decades of European cycling history. In the United States in the early 1970s, when the bike boom began, CONI was the only source for information about proper fit.

The formulas worked fine for some riders, but they created big problems for others. The problem was that the CONI manual's guidelines were geared toward a very specific audience: young, lean, Italian males of Italian national team caliber. So those fit formulas worked, but only for a very small segment of the cyclists from western Europe and North America just coming into the sport during the bike boom of the 1970s. The CONI target audience was well served by these parameters, but older riders, women, those with preexisting injuries, and those carrying a little extra weight struggled to force their bodies into a position that a skinny, young, athletic rider could tolerate quite well.

Position on the bike is always a matter of fitting the bike to the body, not forcing the body to adjust to the bike. So when the demographics of cyclists expanded, individual differences among that larger pool of riders made the old traditional fit methods obsolete. And the bike fit information in this book is a synopsis of what we've learned in the past thirty-five years as experts tried to get riders with many different body shapes and fitness levels to be comfortable on their bikes.

THE FOOT/SHOE/PEDAL INTERFACE

What's true of bike fit for the body as a whole is even more applicable to the feet and the design of cycling shoes.

Just as everyone has a different body type, so everyone has slightly different feet. Feet vary a lot, especially in the way the sole angles when the leg is hanging straight down and the foot dangles free. Sometimes, the soles are parallel to the floor in this situation, while other feet slant one way or the other. If the forefoot is angled from the big toe joint downward to the little toe, as viewed from the rear, it is called varus. If the forefoot angles downward from the small toe to the big toe, it's valgus (see Figure 18.1).

About 90 percent of people have a varus forefoot. A varus foot is perfect for the walking gait. It complements pronation, which is good for shock absorption and propulsion as long as it's not excessive. But the foot is made for walking, not cycling. It's not a rigid structure. Instead it's basically a bag of bones. Forefoot varus causes a loss of power when pedaling. The varus foot collapses against the pedal platform. The shinbone rotates internally. The knee moves repetitively in (medially toward the top tube), robbing power and sometimes causing overuse injuries.

Feet also have a longitudinal arch. This arch is also a perfect design for walking and running because it functions like a leaf spring, storing and

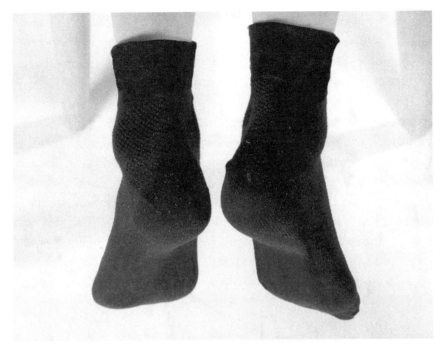

FIGURE 18.1 Forefoot varus as observed from a kneeling position.

returning energy each time you plant your foot and spring off. But on the bike, this design backfires. The foot still collapses on the power stroke, but the energy is returned at the wrong time—on the backstroke where it doesn't help power the pedal stroke.

Therefore, well-designed cycling shoes need a stiff sole to shore up the arch. In the old days, cycling shoe soles were flexible leather. Manufacturers tried to stiffen the sole with a spring steel plate or a wide steel platform attached to the nail-on cleat. Later, manufacturers used wood for the soles of cycling shoes in their quest for stiffness. As you can imagine, this added weight to the shoes. Today, high-end shoes feature extremely lightweight carbon in the soles, adding the necessary stiffness without additional weight.

But in addition to having stiff soles, cycling shoes also need to compensate for the forefoot varus that, remember, is a feature of the feet of

90 percent of the cycling population. This can be done with the Body Geometry varus wedge or cycling orthotics, or with custom orthotics.

To appreciate how a stiff sole and a varus wedge work together to transfer more power to the pedal, picture a rider from the front (see Figure 18.2). Watch his knees during the pedal stroke. The leg is a piston, transferring power from the engine (quads, glutes, cardiovascular system) to the foot and pedal. If the rider's foot is stable and his varus forefoot is supported properly, the knee will track straight up and down. The knee won't wobble in, toward the top tube, or out, away from the bike during the downstroke. Imagine a car's piston that wasn't straight. Power transfer would be terrible—and so would the knocking noise!

The varus wedge puts the foot in a neutral position through the entire pedal stroke. It allows the knee to travel in a nearly vertical line, eliminating side-to-side movement. Again looking at the rider from the front, a

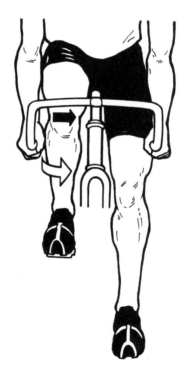

FIGURE 18.2 When power is applied to the pedal, the foot flattens, the shinbone internally rotates, and the knee moves toward the top tube.

plumb line dropped from the head of the thighbone (inside of the hip) and through the middle of the knee would fall to the second toe.

Cycling-specific orthotics fit into the shoes to provide the varus wedge that most riders need. Or, correctly fitted, they can support the much less common valgus foot as well. However, orthotics designed for cyclists are different than those designed for runners. Good cycling orthotics are forefoot posted because cycling is a sport that uses mostly the front of the foot. The orthotics should extend at least to the back of the toes; some are the full length of the shoe. Specialized offers a modular insole worn inside the shoe, which allows cyclists to pick and choose the forefoot and heel pieces separately from a variety of arch supports and forefoot wedges.

However, it's better to build varus corrections into the shoe rather than add them later in the form of orthotics. That's why the Body Geometry line of cycling shoes I designed for Specialized features a varus wedge along with a stiff carbon sole design that includes arch contours that support the longitudinal and metartarsal arches.

In a high-end bike fit, the technician would help you fit the shoe properly. You can also do it yourself by basing your choice of arch supports and forefoot wedges on comfort.

Sometimes, however, riders have biomechanical problems that orthotics can't correct. In that case it may be necessary to make adjustments to the bike's crankset. The best resource for this is Tom Slocum at High Sierra Cycles (on the Web at www.hscycle.com).

Once you get bike fit properly and your feet aligned correctly on the pedal, you can begin to think about the biomechanics of your pedal stroke.

THE BIOMECHANICS OF THE PEDAL STROKE

For most of the century or more that humans have ridden bikes, we didn't know very much about the pedaling motion or the forces that are exerted at different points in the pedal stroke. Without the technology of high-speed cameras to help them, riders and coaches tried to eyeball the spinning foot. They used this plus feedback from their bodies—in the form of pain in their quads—to guess what was going on.

From this, researchers deduced that skilled cyclists pushed down hard on the downstroke while at the same time they pulled up on the backstroke. It seemed like a logical conclusion based on watching cyclists legendary for their smooth pedaling, like five-time Tour de France winner Jacques Anquetil. Of course he pulled up at the back of the pedal stroke. How else could he time trial so fast with so little obvious show of exertion?

Pulling up was assumed to be crucial to fast riding—it unloaded the pedal, assuring that not only was the "rear" foot not going along for the ride while the other foot was trying to push down on the power stroke, it was also adding to the total power transferred to the pedal.

Because of advancing technology and the development of new ways to observe and measure biomechanics in action, we know a great deal about the pedal stroke. And one of the things we know is that even the best pedaling stylists don't produce power when they pull up on the backstroke. The most they can hope for is to unweight the rear foot so it adds less drag to the power output of the foot that is pushing downward. But it's not possible even to get the back foot out of the way entirely.

Sophisticated force-measuring pedals can tell us exactly what forces are being exerted during the pedal stroke and at what angles. Biomechanists like Jeff Broker, Ph.D., developed early models at UCLA in the 1980s. At the Boulder Center for Sports Medicine, we devised our own force-measuring pedals to help the 1996 U.S. Olympic pursuit team hone their skills.

So what *is* going on when we pedal? Cycling biomechanists often use a so-called clock diagram to illustrate the forces involved in pedaling.

As you can see in the clock diagram, these biomechanical findings are complicated and technical (see Figure 18.3). For the purposes of this book, I'll offer a simplified version. Call it the layperson's guide to pedaling mechanics. Here's what we've learned.

Pedaling Is a Restrictive Athletic Motion

The pedaling motion takes place through a relatively small range of motion. If you're using 170 mm crank arms, the legs move in a circle with a diameter of only 340 mm—less than 14 inches. Contrast that to the huge mobility required by basketball players, gymnasts, or triple jumpers.

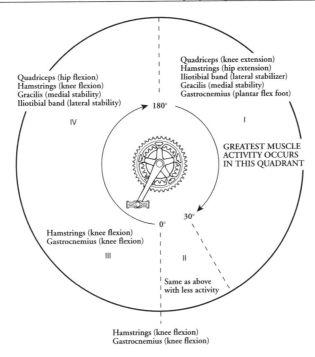

FIGURE 18.3 Biomechanics use a "clock" diagram to illustrate the forces of pedaling.

So while cycling is less likely to cause muscle pulls due to excessive motion, a stretching program is crucial since the muscles aren't stretched in their daily routine of pedaling.

As we saw in the section of this book on bike fit, the bicycle is a fixed machine that can be adjusted by such means as raising or lowering the saddle and changing the reach to the handlebars. Humans are also machines, and while adjustment isn't possible (short of an operation to lengthen your femurs), the human body is adaptable.

The Foot Rarely Pushes Straight Down on the Pedal

The only point at which the foot is pushing straight down is at about the 3 o'clock position, as you can see from the clock diagram. The rest of the time, force is applied tangentially to the pedal, increasing shearing force and reducing the percentage of power from the quads that's actually applied to the bike's forward motion. One of the most important reasons that Specialized included arch contours in the shoe sole is to support the foot when the power transfer is tangential rather than straight up and down. This keeps the foot from sliding forward in the shoe.

Fast Pedaling Lowers Force, Slow Pedaling Increases It

Lance Armstrong has made it popular once again to climb at a fast cadence. He and his coach, Chris Carmichael, know that low-cadence pedaling (60 to 80 rpm) requires large muscular forces, while fast cadences (around 100 rpm) lessen the load on the quads and transfer it to the cardiovascular system. Because the quads fatigue faster, and recover more slowly, than the heart, it makes sense to train your cardiovascular and neuromuscular systems to pedal rapidly.

The Best Cyclists Don't Produce Power When They Pull Up on the Backstroke

As mentioned earlier, force-measuring pedals show us that no cyclists, not even track pursuiters who are capable of silky-smooth pedal strokes at 130 rpm, really exert upward force when the pedal is coming up from dead bottom center.

Mountain Bikers Most Closely Approach the "Ideal" Pedal Stroke

How could it be that mountain bikers get closest to the ideal pedal stroke? We tend to think of mountain bikers using a forceful, hammering pedal stroke as they ride up technical climbs.

But in fact, riding loose surfaces and steep climbs requires an extremely smooth pedal stroke. If the rider emphasizes the downstroke, the surge of power applied to the rear wheel causes it to lose traction on sand and gravel trails.

This phenomenon is painfully evident on Moab's fabled Slickrock Trail. The surface isn't loose; rather, it's smooth sandstone that provides incredible grip to the tires. So it's possible to climb insanely steep pitches—but only if you avoid any power surges to the rear wheel. The slightest jerkiness in the pedal stroke breaks loose the rear wheel and causes a painful slide down the "slick rock."

Getting your skin rubbed off by Utah sandstone provides instant feedback, teaching skilled off-roaders to apply power all the way around the pedal stroke. They still can't pull up, unless they're pedaling at a very low rpm, but they come close.

Even Though There's No Such Thing as a
Perfect Pedal Stroke, It's Still a Goal to Work Toward

You can improve your pedal stroke by doing the following drills.

Concentrate on the top and bottom of the pedal stroke. At around 90 to 120 rpm the pedaling motion is so rapid it's nearly impossible to focus on and modify the different parts of the stroke. The feet simply go around too fast. The trick is to anticipate the motion you want and initiate it early. That means starting the upward pull of the pedal when the pedal is at dead bottom center and initiating the downward push as the pedal comes over the top and begins its descent.

Greg LeMond first described pulling through at the bottom of the stroke saying it's "like scraping the mud off your shoe." The image still works. But pulling through at the bottom is only half the story. You should also concentrate on pushing the knee toward the handlebars as it comes over the top and begins the power phase of the stroke.

By starting both motions well before you want their actions to take effect, you're assured that by the time your command is sent from your brain to your legs, they'll do the right thing at the appropriate time.

Do one-leg pedaling drills. Set your bike on a trainer and warm up. Then unclip one foot and rest it on the rear trainer support or on a chair or stool. Pedal with the other foot, emphasizing good form. The switch feet and repeat. Start by doing several sets of one minute for each leg in a low gear, and increase to sets of five minutes and larger gears.

One-leg pedaling forces you to pedal all the way around the stroke. It will be awkward at first, but with practice you'll improve rapidly. And the pedaling efficiency you acquire will transfer to normal two-leg pedaling on the road.

Ride rollers. Most cyclists now use indoor trainers, but old-school rollers—like a treadmill for bikes—can help you improve pedal form. The reason is that it takes a smooth stroke to even ride the things!

If you pedal awkwardly on rollers, you'll weave all over the rollers or be unable to stay upright. Rollers are the ultimate biofeedback device for smooth pedaling.

Ride off-road. As I mentioned earlier, riding loose-surfaced, steep climbs on a mountain bike is a great way to work on your pedal stroke. You don't have to live in the mountains to get the benefits of this pedaling workout. Even short climbs are helpful.

CHAPTER 19

STRETCHING AND REHABILITATION

In Chapter 5 I talked about knee problems and how they benefit from specific exercises. Generally, if you suffer from knee pain, it's better to let your physical therapist show you how to do these exercises and tailor them to your unique needs. However, several exercises are useful for anyone with mild symptoms or as a preventative measure.

A common theme throughout this book has been the importance of flexibility. Cycling puts the upper body in a fixed position, and the legs' range of motion is limited by the length of the cranks. But flexibility is important—especially as we age—to avoid injury and allow us to get into a comfortable but aerodynamic position on the bike.

Because of this, all cyclists should consider doing simple exercises to stretch regularly and forestall the possibility of patellofemoral pain. You likely are very busy and may barely be able to find time to ride, much less to stretch and add exercises to your routine. So I asked Tami Dick, P.T., CSCS, a bike racer as well as a P.T. and certified strength and conditioning specialist at the Boulder Center for Sports Medicine, to devise a simple routine with just a few exercises and stretches that anyone can fit into a busy schedule.

STRETCHING

For cyclists, the crucial stretches are for the hamstrings, quads, and IT band. If you have issues with other areas—such as tightness in your shoulders—see a physical therapist to learn specific stretches. But for most riders, these are the key muscles that need good movement.

Hamstrings

Flexibility in the hamstrings translates to a decreased risk of low back pain in cyclists and may allow a lower, more aerodynamic torso angle. To stretch your hamstrings (see Figure 19.1):

- Stand in front of a step that's 4 to 8 inches high. Put your heel on the step with the knee slightly bent and your toes up.
- Hinge forward from the hips. Don't bend your back. Straighten your knee on the extended leg.

Hold the stretch for 30 to 45 seconds. Repeat 3 to 4 times. You can do this stretch 2 to 3 times a day for best results.

FIGURE 19.1 Hamstring stretch.

Iliotibial Band (Lateral Hip Drop)

A tight IT band frequently leads to lateral knee pain in cyclists, due to friction caused by the repetitive nature of the pedal stroke. To avoid this tightness, do the following stretches (see Figure 19.2):

- Stand next to a wall with the painful knee toward the wall. Place your forearm on that same side against the wall. For example, if the right knee is sore, place your right forearm against the wall.

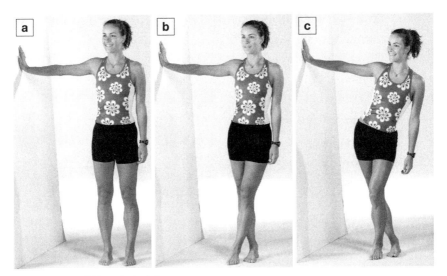

FIGURE 19.2 IT band stretch.

- Cross the other leg over the leg with the painful knee so the feet are about 6 to 8 inches apart. (In this example, you would place your left leg over your right leg.)
- Cave your hips toward the wall until you feel a good stretch. Keep your shoulders away from the wall with the outstretched elbow.
- Hold the stretch for 30 to 45 seconds. Repeat 3 to 4 times. You can do this stretch 2 to 3 times a day for best results.

Quadriceps

Tightness in the quadriceps increases the compressive forces on the patella into the femur, which can lead to pain. To stretch the quadriceps (see Figure 19.3):

- Lie on your stomach. Bend one knee so your heel moves toward your butt.
- Loop a towel or strap around your ankle and hold the strap in the same hand as the leg you're trying to stretch.
- Pull your heel gently toward your butt.

- Hold this gentle stretch for 5 seconds, then push against the pressure of the towel or strap for 5 seconds and repeat the stretch.
- Do 3 to 5 cycles of this stretch-contract-stretch pattern.

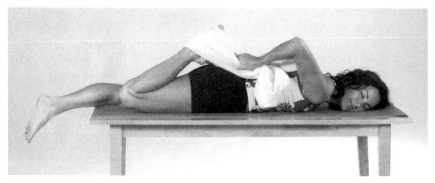

FIGURE 19.3 Self-assisted quad- and hip-flexor stretches.

PATELLOFEMORAL (KNEE) EXERCISES

Side-Lying Glute Medius Clamshell

A strong glute medius helps control leg rotation, maintaining the alignment of the knee over the foot through the pedal stroke. To strengthen this muscle (see Figure 19.4):

- Lie on your side with the side you want to strengthen up. Keep your pelvis vertical and point your hip bone to the ceiling.
- Bend the knees 90 degrees or greater. Stack the legs together, knees and feet touching.
- Open the legs by moving the upper knee toward the ceiling about a foot above the knee that's on the ground. Hinge at the hip and ankle. Don't move the pelvis.
- Add resistance by using a Thera-Band or other elastic band.
- Do this movement continually for 1 minute, 1 to 2 times per day.

This movement also strengthens muscles that provide stability when you're riding out of the saddle.

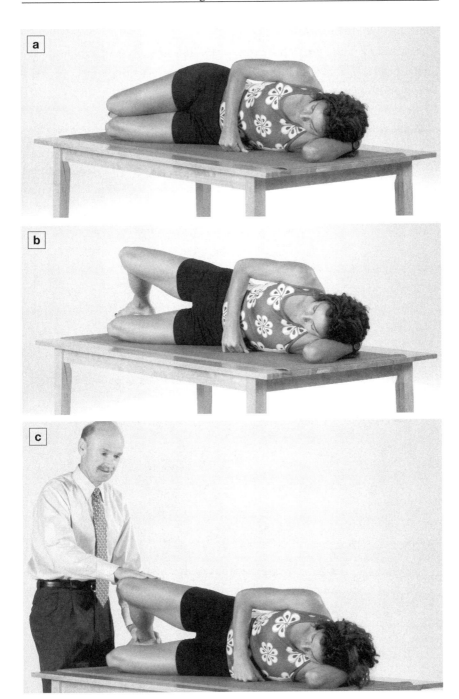

FIGURE 19.4 Side-lying glute-medius clamshell.

Short Arc Quad Extensions

The vastus medialis portion of the quadriceps actively controls how the patella tracks in the knee. Strengthen this muscle to prevent knee pain with the following stretch (see Figure 19.5):

- Sit on the floor with your back against a wall and legs extended.
- Place a rolled-up towel (6 to 8 inches in diameter) under one knee.

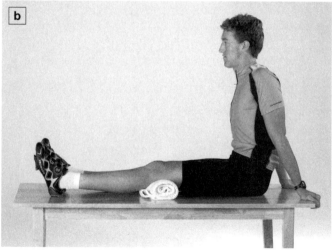

FIGURE 19.5 Short-arc quad extensions.

- Tighten your vastus medalis (the pear-shaped muscle on the inside and just above the knee) while pushing the back of your knee into the towel roll. Keeping the vastus medialis tight, raise the heel off the floor and straighten the knee.
- Lower the heel, keeping the vastus medialis tight.

Begin with 15 repetitions and work up to 50 repetitions, 3 times a day.

Chair Press
This exercise strengthens both the VMO, the vastus medialis oblique or the inner part of the quads, and the glutes (see Figure 19.6).

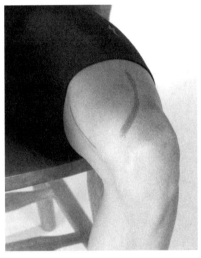

- Sit on a straight chair with your feet flat on the floor and your hips and knees at 90 degrees.
- Push the feet into the floor, isometrically contracting the quads. In other words, tense the muscle as if you're trying to stand up. This "sets" the muscles so the patella is held in place and doesn't hurt.
- Hold this position for 5 seconds and then relax.
- Do 3 to 4 sets of 15 repetitions throughout the day or every time you get out of a chair.

FIGURE 19.6 Chair press with lines marking the vastus medialis of the right knee.

CHAPTER 20

WHAT WE
DON'T KNOW
(BUT I WISH WE DID!)

IN THIS BOOK I'VE DETAILED THE LATEST INFORMATION IN SPORTS medicine and biomechanics as it relates to the cyclist. I've gleaned this knowledge from research, from my professional colleagues, and from personal experience gained in more than 150,000 career miles on the bike along with two world championship titles. However, the best information has come from thirty years of clinical experience, working every day with cyclists, ranging from recreational riders to the best riders in the world. I've seen nearly every cycling malady, fit problem, and traumatic injury that it's possible to incur.

But there's still a lot we don't know about how the human body and the bike work together. It would make my job a lot easier if sports science and medical researchers could come up with the answers!

It can be frustrating for cyclists, too, who have questions and look to their coaches for answers, when their coaches can't give a definitive answer. To clarify the issues that still remain to be solved, and to prompt bright young researchers to turn their attention to these problems—and maybe even encourage grant-awarding institutions to come up with the money—I've compiled a list of things we don't know.

CAN WE HELP AGING
ATHLETES RIDE BETTER?

As we saw in Chapter 16, consistent and intense exercise can dramatically slow the rate of age-related performance losses. Study subjects who actually increased their maximum oxygen intake, or VO_2max, in the years after age 45 were blessed with great genes as well as a sturdy work ethic. Not everyone can be as fit and fast at age 60 as they were in their thirties.

But some of the aging athletes I see in my practice can't train intensely even though they'd love to do so. Various ailments, ranging from bad backs, failing hearts, rickety hips, and arthritic knees, keep them from riding their bikes as much as they'd like, much less racking up lots of miles or grinding out the sort of white-hot interval sessions that we now know can forestall most performance loss. And many of the older athletes I encounter don't care about beating the 20-year-olds up the hill. They just want to keep riding.

As I approach my mid-fifties, I sympathize with these eager but hurting riders. The mind is willing but the skeletal structure, tendons, or ligaments are weak. These riders have the verve and enthusiasm of youngsters—but the chassis of a 1950 VW Beetle.

So first on my list of needed medical advancements are techniques that will restore bodily function to those who, through neglect or overuse or previous injuries, are unable to reap the benefits of riding as hard as they'd like. We need better artificial hips and knees, better prostheses for those who have lost limbs, better methods of controlling ailments like tendinitis, ACL injuries, and low back pain. Once we can guarantee structural soundness, then riders could train hard into their nineties and beyond.

HOW DOES THE HEART REACT TO
LONG-TERM ENDURANCE EXERCISE?

In essence, for the first time in human history, people are doing hard endurance exercise for their whole lives, living as long as eighty or ninety years. In the past, people didn't do endurance exercise after their sporting careers were ended in their twenties or early thirties. Or they did hard physical labor on the farm, but it wasn't aerobic. Or they simply didn't live very long if their aerobic exercise consisted of running from saber-toothed-tigers and cave bears.

But our generation is the first to work hard aerobically for thirty or forty years straight. And we have no idea how the body and heart react to such strain over a long time period. So all long-term endurance athletes are in a sense guinea pigs on this new frontier in physiology.

All the authorities agree that this is a fertile area for studies. They just haven't been done yet in any quantity. One area in which there are a few studies is in atrial fibrillation, a condition in which the two upper chambers of the heart quiver instead of beating normally. The studies show a slightly increased risk of atrial fibrillation among long-term endurance athletes, but they don't yet know why.

WHAT'S THE BEST STANCE WIDTH?

Although many riders don't realize it, the width of your feet while pedaling can vary markedly depending on factors like the width of the bottom bracket shell, the length of the bottom bracket axle, pedal design, and the way the cleat is placed on the sole of the shoe.

This stance width is often called "Q angle," but that's a misnomer. Q angle as anatomists use the term has to do with the angle of the femur in relation to the knee. It has little in common with how wide apart your feet are while you're pedaling.

At first glance, it seems that a narrower stance on the pedals would be better than a wide stance because narrower means more aerodynamic. In fact, I supervised studies before the 1996 Olympics to determine the best stance width for U.S. National Team pursuit riders. We found that a narrow stance did indeed improve performance, and the top riders turned out to be those whose physical attributes allowed them to ride with the pedals close together. In short, our Olympic pursuit team had to be knock-kneed and flat-footed with excessive pronation!

But the pursuit is a special case, involving just a few minutes of intense riding. So for recreational cyclists or road racers, what's the best stance width? This has yet to be determined. The answer is important for pedal and bottom bracket design, as well as for bike design since the bottom bracket shell might have to be modified.

It's also important for designing crank arms. Many riders, especially those who pronate excessively, often bang their ankle bones on the crank. To avoid this they move their cleats to the inside of their shoe soles, thus moving their shoes (and ankle bones) out as far from the crank as possible. This moves their ankles sufficiently far from the cranks to avoid contact, but at a cost—doing so widens their stance, sometimes leading to injury.

But if a narrow stance is found to be most effective, component manufacturers will need to design cranks that allow a narrow stance without interfering with the pedal stroke.

WHAT IS THE MOST EFFECTIVE
FOOT POSITION ON THE PEDAL?

Traditionally, cleats have been positioned to put the ball of the foot directly over the middle of the pedal axle. Riders positioned this way can pedal on the balls of their feet, exactly as if they were running and pushing off powerfully from the forefoot.

But researchers are not sure that running is analogous to cycling in this regard. As we saw in Chapter 7, the foot is an unstable structure, and when the considerable forces generated by the quads and glutes are transferred through the foot to the pedal, the foot often moves, absorbing some of your hard-won power.

The body realizes this. Suppose you didn't have cleats but were riding instead on flat pedals with tennis shoes and your foot was free to migrate to its most efficient position on the pedal. In that case, feet about a men's size 9 would tend to naturally end up with the ball of the foot over the pedal axle, smaller feet would automatically move back on the pedal to give the foot more leverage, and larger feet would tend to slide forward on the pedal to provide more stability.

But beyond this, we don't have a good quantified study to show the relationships among power production, different foot positions, and varying foot sizes.

And the issue is complicated by the tendency for the nerves between the metatarsal bones to get irritated by the repetitive nature of pedaling. One way to alleviate this so-called hot foot (see Chapter 7) is by moving the cleat to the rear of the shoe, taking pressure off the forefoot area. As we've seen, ultralong-distance riders often drill their shoes to get the cleat even farther back. Now if we just knew how much power gain or loss such a modification entails. Scientists?

WHAT'S THE SOLUTION TO LOW BACK PROBLEMS?

Back problems are the leading complaint among patients who visit neurologists and orthopedists. The same complaint is among the top ten reasons people schedule an appointment with any kind of physician. Back pain is more likely to send you to your doctor than having a fever, a rash, or a pain in your knee.

Some excellent studies show that more than 70 percent of adults suffer back pain at some time in their lives. Yet new studies question whether many of the commonly used treatments do any good. In fact, some experts say that in 85 percent of cases in which a patient suffers from back pain, it is impossible to say why their back hurts, even with an array of X-rays and MRIs. What's even more mysterious, severe back pain sometimes vanishes without specific intervention.

Cycling generally helps alleviate back pain. But depending on the type of pain and what caused it (if that can be determined), suffering riders may have to change their position on the bike. Specifically, many victims of back pain must raise their handlebars, sometimes significantly higher than their saddles, to be able to ride comfortably. This upright position is neither aerodynamic nor stylish. And it can interfere with power production as well. So we need to know a lot more about back pain—its causes, treatment, and prevention.

WHAT ARE THE EFFECTS OF ROCKING TORQUE?

You may not have heard much about rocking torque, but it could be significantly altering the amount of power you're able to produce. It also has ramifications for pedal design as well as for riders with enough leg length inequality to require that they use a shim between their cleat and shoe sole.

Think of rocking torque as the power that's lost when the foot has to stabilize a pedal platform that's higher than the pedal axle. If we could somehow put the sole of the foot directly in contact with the center of the pedal spindle, there'd be no rocking torque. All power would go directly into pushing the pedal around.

But suppose we position the sole of the foot above the center of the pedal axle—with shoe soles of various thicknesses, orthotics, footbeds, and the pedal platform itself. Then the pedal tends to rock forward when we push down on it. Power that would normally be used to turn the cranks is siphoned off by the energy needed to hold the foot steady and overcome this tendency of the pedal to turn over.

The reason this happens is that the foot doesn't push straight down on the pedal. Instead there's a forward force on the pedal platform as the foot comes over the top of the stroke. The higher the platform above the middle of the spindle, the greater the tendency of the pedal to roll forward when force is applied.

At one end of the spectrum is the hypothetical pedal with no rocking torque—the sole of the foot is "on" the center of the pedal spindle. At the other end is a flat pedal with a six-inch block of wood to build up the platform. You couldn't pedal it—the pedal would flop over when you applied force. But exactly how much "stack height" is acceptable? How much power are we losing when we choose a pedal with 1 cm of platform height over the middle of the pedal axle compared to one with only 8 mm?

We don't know the answer to these questions, and they're important. If rocking torque turns out to be a significant power thief, pedal and shoe manufacturers will want to come up with innovative designs to combat it. And if it is a major factor, designers would also want to help those riders who, because of a leg length discrepancy, need to shim up one cleat to avoid injury. Perhaps this could be done with innovative crank designs.

WHAT POSITION PRODUCES THE OPTIMUM TRADE-OFF BETWEEN POWER PRODUCTION AND AERODYNAMICS?

Cyclists have gotten much faster in time trials over the past fifteen years, and arguably, this increase in speed has been made possible by the invention of aero bars, which allow more aerodynamic rider positions than regular handlebars.

Compare the frontal profile that the wind "saw" when Eddy Merckx set the World Hour Record in 1972 riding a conventional steel track bike with standard drop bars to the frontal profile of a modern time trialist like 2003 World Champion David Millar on a bike with aerodynamic tubes and bars.

Not only are the newer bikes more aerodynamic in themselves, their low front ends allow the rider to get lower while the aero bars encourage riders to position their arms very close together. The result is a "slippery" rider profile in the wind and increases in speed—for a given power output—on the order of several miles per hour.

But getting low and narrow brings with it several penalties as well. Some comfort is sacrificed, but for time trials up to an hour in duration, this isn't a big factor. Trying to maintain more than 90 percent of your maximum heart rate for forty kilometers produces enough pain to blot out the discomfort of the low position! More significant is the reduced bike handling that accompanies a very low body position and narrow hand placement. Even the best-designed time trial bike doesn't handle like a conventional road bike, and time trialists have to ride many miles "in the position" to feel comfortable in corners or strong crosswinds.

But the biggest potential drawback of a time trial position is that it can sap power output. As the rider's shoulders go down and the back approaches horizontal, the saddle has to be moved forward. This opens up the hip angle so the thighs don't hit the ribcage on each pedal stroke. But moving the saddle forward, to a position quite different from the normal road position where most of a rider's training is done, can severely limit power.

And pro cyclists must also contend with a rule by the Union Cycliste Internationale (or UCI, the authority that regulates international cycling) that states that the nose of the saddle must be at least 5 cm behind the bottom bracket. This limits how far over the bottom bracket riders can position their hips and, thus, how low they can get without their quads impinging on their chests.

The question is: At what point is the increased aerodynamic efficiency of a low position negated by the resulting reduction in power output? We can determine what position is best for each rider in expensive and time-consuming wind tunnel tests. But we don't know if that ideal aerodynamic position allows us to produce enough power to meet our goals.

So where's the trade-off between aerodynamics and power production? At what point do the curves of falling power production and rising aerodynamic benefits intersect? That's the real secret to getting the most out of your ability in time trials. Although we can make some rough estimates by using a power meter on a flat and windless road, we don't know a simple and effective method of finding out for sure.

EXACTLY HOW MUCH TRAINING SHOULD WE DO EACH DAY TO PRODUCE MAXIMUM GAINS?

Proper training load has traditionally been determined based on a combination of markers like morning heart rate, perceptions of fatigue or vigor, and plain old guesswork. The trick is applying exactly the right training stimulus to create improvement without resulting in burnout, overtraining, or poor performance.

As any experienced cyclist knows, this is devilishly difficult.

If we follow the training programs of top cyclists, instead of becoming as fast as they are, we find instead that we can't do the workouts at all. The training that allows Lance Armstrong to win the Tour de France would put most of us in intensive care.

We can try the scientific method, monitoring our recovery with resting heart rate, cortisol levels, and frequent performance testing. But these markers often contradict themselves. Resting heart rate may say we're good to go, while performance is suffering a precipitous slide. Or we use perceived exertion—a rating scale for our workouts that promises to tell us when to ride hard, when to ride easy, when to rest. But cycling attracts goal-oriented, driven people who often ignore their feelings of fatigue and pain in order to push themselves to train harder.

The fact is that researchers have been unable to find a simple test that shows whether you have recovered from past training or competition and are ready for more hard efforts. So determining training loads is often a bit like magic—more intuition than science—relying on canny guesses by the athlete or coach. If we had a simple test that could tell us exactly how hard to train—or rest—on any given day, we'd be able to get the most out of our cycling abilities.

SUGGESTED READING

Burke, Edmund, Ph.D. *High-Tech Cycling.* Champaign, IL: Human Kinetics, 2003.

Burke, Edmund, Ph.D. *Science of Cycling.* Champaign, IL: Human Kinetics, 1988.

Holmes, Jim and Andrew L. Pruitt. "Bicycling Injuries." *Clinics in Sports Medicine* (January 1994).

Phinney, Davis, Connie Carpenter, and Peter Nye. *Training for Cycling: The Ultimate Guide to Improved Performance.* New York: Putnam Publishing Group, 1992.

INDEX

tendinitis, 48–51, 59, 60–61
  Achilles tendon, 76–78
  controlling, 176
  inflammation, 47
  stretching and, 109
Testa, Max, 149
testing, 117, 182
  blood, 121–24
  performance, 117, 118–20, 125, 127–28
  physiological, 117–24, 129
  procedures, 120–21
testosterone, 123–24, 145, 146–47
thyroid stimulating hormone, 123
TIBC (total iron-binding capacity), 122
time trials, 34–35, 66, 181
  simulated, 132
  for testing, 127–28
torque, rocking, 179–80
torso angle, 23, 26–27
trainers, 142
training. *See also* exercise
  aging and, 176
  base, 130
  dimensions of, 128–29
  endurance, 134
  goals, 133
  honesty in, 127
  intensity, 129, 130, 133, 176
  load, 182–83
  metabolism and, 115
  periodization, 130
  personalizing, 125–35
  phases, 130–33
  planning, 121, 129–33, 142
  properly, 106
  returning to, 139
  speed, 135
  volume, 129, 130, 133
  VO$_2$max, 135
  weight, 142
training diary, 107
training zones, 128, 133–35
tube length, 23

unconsciousness, 98–99
Union Cyclists Internationale (UCI), 181
upper respiratory tract infections (URTIs), 138
urethritis, 88, 89

varus wedge, 160–61
vastus medialis, 52, 53, 173
velocity, 119
ventilation, 128
vibration damping, 149, 150
vitamin supplements, 137–38
VO$_2$max, 118, 128
  decline, 141
  increasing, 176
  intervals, 132
  measuring, 120–21
  percent of, 119
  training, 135
von Hooydonck, Edwig, 152

warming up, 62, 109, 120, 133
wattage output, 119, 128, 129, 131
WBC (white blood cells), 105, 123
weather, 133
weight bearing, 45
weight distribution, 25

ABOUT THE AUTHORS

Andrew L. Pruitt, Ed.D., is an internationally-known athletic trainer, physician assistant, and educator. Pruitt is director of the Boulder Center for Sports Medicine in Boulder, Colorado (www.bch.org/sportsmedicine). He is one of the world's foremost experts on bike fit and cycling injuries.

Pruitt headed the U.S. Cycling Federation's sports medicine program for many years, including through four World Championships. He was the Chief Medical Officer for U.S. Cycling at the 1996 Olympics in Atlanta. He also helped design medical coverage for the Atlanta cycling venues on a model he developed as Medical Director of the Tour Dupont. Pruitt is the recognized leader in computerized cycling gait analysis, a technique that uses three-dimensional computer technology to determine perfect bike fit for any rider, a service available at the BCSM.

Andy Pruitt began his athletic career in traditional sports—football, basketball, baseball, and track. Losing the lower part of his right leg in a hunting accident at age 14 didn't stop him. He became a wrestler and high jumper, eventually winning twelve high school varsity letters. He attended Drake University and Iowa State, earning a Bachelor of Science degree in anatomy, an M.S. from the University of Colorado, and an Ed.D. from California Coast University. He became an athletic trainer at the University of Colorado in 1973 and served for many years as Director of Sports Medicine.

While at CU, Pruitt began cycling and skiing. He won a bronze medal in the downhill at the U.S. Disabled Ski Championships in 1978, but found his true passion in cycling. Over a ten-year racing career, he earned a USCF Category 2 ranking competing against able-bodied riders. He won two national championships and two world championships as a disabled rider. He continues to compete in time trials and occasional road races. As late as 2001 he had a top-ten finish among able-bodied racers in the 50+ category of the Durango-to-Silverton Road Race.

Andy's wife, Sue, and son, Scott, are avid cyclists and skiers. Scott is a past national-caliber junior Nordic skier and now an aspiring U23 road racer honing his skills by racing in Belgium.

Fred Matheny has written about cycling for twenty-eight years, including five books and hundreds of articles. Matheny first met Pruitt on top of the infamous "wall" of the Morgul-Bismark road race course outside Boulder, Colorado, while they were watching a late-1970s edition of the legendary Red Zinger Classic. Since then, they have collaborated on dozens of articles and ridden countless miles together.

Matheny began cycling in the early 1970s after an athletic career that included football and track in high school and football at Baldwin-Wallace College in Ohio, where he was named all-league and his team's outstanding offensive lineman. After he moved to Colorado in 1970, cycling helped him lose fifty pounds he had gained to play college ball. He enjoyed riding so much that it soon became his passion.

Matheny rode his first race in 1976. A Category 2 racer since 1978, his top placings include a Cat. 3 win in the Mount Evans Hill Climb; a world record of 5 days, 11 hours in the 1996 Team Race Across America; first place in the Colorado Masters Time Trial Championships 1997 and 2003; and third place at the 2000 Masters National Time Trial Championships.

Matheny and his wife of thirty-seven years, Debbie, live in Montrose, Colorado. Their son, Ross, and his wife, Laura, are teachers in the Seattle area.